Sidetracked
Home
Executives™

Sidetracked Home Executives™

From Pigpen to Paradise

By Pam Young and Peggy Jones

Edited by Sydney Craft Rozen

WARNER BOOKS

A Time Warner Company

WARNER BOOKS EDITION

Copyright © 1977, 1978, 1979, 1981, 2001
    by Pamela I. Young and Peggy A. Jones

Sidetracked Home Executive® is a federally registered mark of Sidetracked Home Executive, Inc.

Warner Books, Inc., 1271 Avenue of the Americas, New York, NY 10020
Visit our Web site at www.twbookmark.com

W A Time Warner Company

Printed in the United States of America
First Printing: September 1981
Revised and Updated Edition: February 2001
10 9 8 7 6 5 4 3 2

Library of Congress Cataloging-in-Publication Data
Young, Pam (Pamela I.)
    Sidetracked home executives : from pigpen to paradise / by Pam Young and
    Peggy Jones : edited by Sydney Craft Rozen.
        p. cm.
    ISBN 0-446-67767-1
    1.) Home economics.   2. Homemakers—Time management.   I.
Jones, Peggy (Peggy A.)   II. Rozen, Sydney Craft.   III. Title.

TX158. Y62 2001
640—dc21   00-044920

Book design by Tom Nozkowski
Cover design by Elaine Groh

Dedicated with love to Fred

Special Thanks

Special thanks to DANNY, MICHAEL, PEGGY, CHRIS, JOANNA, JEFFREY, and ALLY, and especially to the memory of our mom and dad. Without their love and support, this book would not have been possible.

Acknowledgments

To Jim Shinn, our cartoonist, who came to our rescue because he loved our mom and dad.

To the twenty-two students who attended our first class in Vancouver, Washington. They were evidence that our problem was shared by other women.

To our agent John Boswell, whose incredible persistence changed our minds.

To Molly Lee, the Webmaster of our Web site at www.shesintouch.com. Molly is able to take our thoughts and send them into cyberspace in style. Together with her talent and understanding of S.H.E.s, Molly has built a fun-loving, informative, and comfortable home for sidetracked sisters to find support.

To the countless women who visit us on the Internet. You offer your collective wisdom, glean from each other's inspiration, and encourage us to continue our work.

—

Women like you are the reason we have succeeded in business for more than two decades without having keen business minds.

To the Web site mentors for all their effort and support: Wacky Woman, Sgt. McD, Flylady, Webwoman, and Unity.

To the faithful subscribers of our tape-of-the-month club, "Pam and Peggy Keeping in Touch". You are our extended family. You have laughed and cried with us and kept us afloat through the lean years by purchasing every product we ever created. Like our mom filled the freezer with Girl Scout cookies, you have supported all of our efforts from the beginning.

To the Sidetracked Sisterhood of women across the country who are selflessly committed to helping other women get and stay organized. Using the Sidetracked Home Executive Systems, these caring volunteers are commissioned yearly to lead a series of meetings in their home. They share their experiences and offer one-on-one guidance and encouragement. With their help, we reach thousands more women than we ever could on our own.

Contents

—

Introduction

We have a feeling that the system in this book is an answer to your prayers. We wanted our book to be from us to you, and the only way to have it be exactly what we are was to write it ourselves. We had to call on every ounce of dormant self-discipline we had to finish it. Thanks to a brilliant editor, Sydney Craft Rozen, and a wonderfully gifted cartoonist, Jim Shinn, we are thrilled beyond words to introduce our book, *Sidetracked Home Executives: From Pigpen to Paradise.* It is the first book written on getting organized from a "reformed slob" point of view. Until now, most of the books written on this subject were written by born-organized (B.O.s) people, who do not understand the unique nature of a sidetracked person. On the other hand, if you are a B.O. and have to live with someone like us (because you are his or her parent, spouse, child, or sibling), this book will help you to understand and cope with your dilemma.

Men who find themselves in the role of full-time home-maker need this book. Through countless interviews with men who are single dads, we can wholeheartedly understand the frustration of trying to keep a happy home, in addition to the responsibilities outside the home.

We recommend that you read this book once all the way through, to get the wonderful feeling that you are all right, just where you are, no matter how messy and disorganized. Regardless of how chaotic things might be, it's going to be alright.

Then, once you've laughed with us, cried with us, and glimpsed a sense of order, you will be ready to go back to Chapter 4 to set up your own system. Introduced in this book is the entire 3×5 card filing system, which has helped hundreds of thousands of people improve their homes and businesses.

Enjoy this book, as it was meant to make you laugh. Rejoice and know you are not alone . . . that at least two other souls were worse than you. If it worked for them, it will work for anyone! God bless you.

Sidetracked
Home
Executives™

The Way We Used to Be

We wanted to call this chapter "The Way We Were," but, since that's a famous song, we figured we'd have to get permission from the writer and we didn't know his address or even his name. The only way to find out would have been to load all six kids into the station wagon and drive downtown to Leo's Taco & Record Pavilion. (Leo lets you dine to music, and if you buy an album you get two tacos for the price of one.) But we didn't think we should risk it. Knowing how we are, we would have ended up listening to all our favorite records, stuffing ourselves with tacos, and coming home exhausted, with a bagful of albums, indigestion, and no songwriter's name and address. There we'd be—sidetracked again, doing the very thing that had caused our problem in the first place.

So, realizing that Chapter 1's title lacks the class it could have had, we decided to just skip the temptation and move right along to June 16, 1977—the day we both went down for the final count and made up our minds to change.

1

We love knowing the exact day we drew the line. On June 16 we both hit bottom and, since we had no place to go but up, we vowed to master what had controlled us for a lifetime. What someone once said is true: "You will never break free to newness until you are utterly disgusted with the old way." The desire to change, plus the decision to do something about it, is an important event and needs to be remembered and celebrated.

We realized on June 16, 1977, that there must be an answer, and indeed there was.

The events you are about to read are TRUE. OUR NAMES have been changed to protect the innocent. (Has *Dragnet* been off the air long enough to use that line without permission from Sergeant Joe Friday, or do we have to load up the station wagon with the six kids and drive down to the TV station?)

DATE: June 16, 1977
SCENE i. The home of Waynette Crystal

WAYNETTE'S STORY

Ten A.M. I woke up that morning, as I did many mornings, bursting with enthusiasm and ready for some belated spring cleaning. I was just thrilling! I wore my standard cleaning uniform: paint-stained pants, husband's sweatshirt (the same one I'd slept in), a red bandanna, wrinkled beyond recognition, and mukluks. I had that glorious feeling that this would be the day I'd clean the house from top to bottom, and nothing would go unattended. I lined up the children, ages one, three, and four. True, they looked young but, by my standards, capable. . . .

"OK, you guys, today we are going to clean this place up, and THIS TIME it's going to stay that way! You boys, rip the covers off your beds and throw them in the hall. I'll take the drapes down. Chris, get all those pop bottles out from under the sink; we can return them to the store and rent a steam cleaner for the carpets.

"Jeff, see who's at the door. No—tell them you can't play. Allyson, NO! That's cat food, keekee, get out of that. OK, do you all have your work assignments? Where's Jeff? What's that clicking noise?

"Hi, operator. Say, could I get a credit for that last call, the one to Trinidad? There was a little mistake in dialing.

"All right, everybody back in the hall. I'm gonna say this one more time: THE PHONE IS OFF LIMITS. Chris, answer the door. NO! You have work to do. That's right, Jeff, dump out all your drawers; we'll sort everything later. Yeah, you can make a tent out of the sheets, but you can't take that sandwich in there. No, you can't have any chocolate chips; I've gotta bake twenty-five thousand cookies for church tonight. I smell tuna. . . .

"Bring all those boxes up from the basement, and we'll pack some of this junk away. Let's start a garage-sale pile here in the hall. No, we can't sell those; they're library books. OK, just ONE story, but then we've got to get back to work. Once upon a time . . . I DO smell tuna!

"No, see, Allyson, the box with the kitty on it is Gawkie's food; the yellow box is your cereal. See, yellow . . . Y-E-L-L-O-W. . . . Spit 'em out, Ally—ooh, Chris, get Mom a towel! Jeff, go get those flash cards in the junk drawer; we'll go into the tent and teach Ally her colors."

Within two hours the hall was a crazyhouse of pop bottles, library books, miscellaneous garage-sale merchandise, clothes to sort and store, drapes, bedding, old toys, Friskies, Cheerios, chocolate chips, and a choo-choo train of cardboard boxes—not to mention the magnificent tent, where we were all hiding out.

The doorbell rang. Jeff answered it. I screamed from inside the tent, "Check the bottoms of your feet before you walk all over my drapes!" The tent collapsed around us, no doubt from the force and intensity of my command.

A voice like Darth Vader's announced with dignity, "I have checked the bottoms of my feet, and they appear to be clean."

I heard Jeff say cautiously, "You'd better step over this stuff. I think we're movin.'"

Then Darth's voice again: "Is your mother home, lad?"

Listening from under the pile of sheets, I lay motionless, praying that my presence would go undetected. "She's in those sheets," Jeff said. I peeked out from under the fallen tent, embarrassed but grateful for a breath of fresh air, and looked up at my husband's boss.

"Are you moving, Mrs. Shedlester?" he asked. For a moment I thought that might be my best shot. I could be over the border before Barney, my husband, got home from work. But, being a religious person, I felt compelled to tell the truth.

"No, we're not moving," I said as I crawled out from under the rubble. "I'm just cleaning."

Barney's boss smiled a funny smile and backed up two steps. "I came for the key," he said politely, edging toward the door. My husband had put a note on the bulletin board at work, advertising a travel trailer we were trying to sell. The note included our address and instructions: "Drive by and my wife will give you the key."

"The key?" I asked, wild-eyed. The key. Ha! Weeks later I found it under Gawkie's cushion, too late to make the sale.

When Barney's boss drove away, still keyless, I slumped to the floor in the corner at the end of the hall

and surveyed the chaos I had created. I loved being a homemaker, really, truly loved it. How could such a pure motive—wanting a pretty, clean house—turn into this nightmare of confusion and clutter? At what point had I torn up more than I could put back? I realized faintly that NORMAL PEOPLE DON'T CLEAN THIS WAY. I knew if I could just find the phone (the last time I saw it, it was in the tent under a pile of chocolate-smeared flash cards), I could call my sister, and together we'd resolve this problem for all time.

SCENE ii. The home of Mava Dinette, Waynette's sister

MAVA'S STORY

Ten A.M. A massive wave of poetic creativity overcame me this morning. Two hours later I had finished this poem. I called it "The Housewife."

THE HOUSEWIFE

There was a housewife I once knew
Who had so much work that she wanted to do.
She had eight loads of laundry to wash and to dry,
Five beds to make and groceries to buy.
Library books three years overdue,
She thought, "Go to the library? No, let's go to the zoo."
"Hurray!" cried her children. But, alas, they stayed
*   home.*
The eight loads of laundry had all the clothes that they
*   owned.*
She had dishes from dinner the night before
And gum to scrape off the kitchen floor.
And just as she knelt to scrape up the gum,

—

She thought about popcorn and she wanted some.
So she got out the popper; it was full of rice.
And she thought to herself, "It would be nice
To get out the pictures of my wedding dress,"
But she couldn't find them because of the mess
In her living room where she kept a shelf
Full of books on how to improve herself.
So she picked out a book and she sat and she read.
And she thought to herself, "I'll take a nap instead."
So she stretched and she yawned and flopped into bed.
Then she remembered something her husband had said.
So she got out the iron and she looked for his shirt
Which had fallen into a pile of dirt
She had swept in a corner a few days before
And had stopped because someone had knocked at the
    door.
Then she sighed, "Oh dear!" and she moaned, "Poor me!"
And she grabbed a sack of taco chips and turned on the
    TV.
And she watched all the game shows.
And she watched Love of Life.
And she dreamed of becoming the perfect wife!

When my poetic attack had passed on that fateful June day, I was in my new home, lying on the living-room floor, surrounded by 157 Bekins' moving boxes—all marked MISCELLANEOUS. I agonized over the thought of unpacking. I felt alone, guilty, isolated—and abandoned by Bekins. (They made me promise never to call them again.) I wept gently at first and, when that didn't relieve my anguish, I began to heave great, grief-filled sobs. Suddenly my life flashed before me.

I heard the voice of my dear mother: "I don't know

what to do with you girls. I've tried everything to get you to keep things neat and orderly. I give up. Where did I go wrong?" Somewhere in some child-psychology book, she had read that the best way to handle the "messy child" was to close the door to the child's room and allow it to be what it must be. The theory was that after a few days the child would be forced to clean the room, out of necessity and a natural desire for order.

Not true. My sister and I burrowed deeper and deeper into our mounds of clutter, like two little groundhogs. We came out into daylight only for nourishment. So, after experimenting with that theory for three weeks, our immaculate mother burned the book and threw her first SRF (Saturday Room Fit). She lined us up in the hall and, speaking through clenched teeth, said, "OK, you guys, today you're going to clean this place up, and THIS TIME it's going to stay that way...."

I had been using variations on that theme for twelve years with my own kids, and where had it got me? In the middle of the living-room floor, surrounded by 157 unpacked miscellaneous boxes.

In the depths of despair, I heard the faint ringing of my telephone. I staggered through the maze of boxes, frantically searching for the phone and feeling much like one of those rats that scientists watch with delight. I managed to find the phone before it rang for the twenty-seventh time and made a feeble attempt at sounding pert when I answered it.

The voice at the other end was weak and pathetic, but somehow vaguely familiar. "Waynee, is that you?" I asked.

"Oh, Mava," she wailed. "I've gotta get out of this mess!"

We met fifteen minutes later at Eddie's Villa del Wee-

nie (a Mexican hot-dog restaurant) to examine the root of our problem. We somehow found strength in knowing we weren't totally alone; at least we had each other. For hours we sat at Eddie's, sharing horror stories and admitting the gross inadequacies of our lives as sidetracked stay-at-home moms.

We were pleasantly shocked by the similarities of our true confessions. We were *both* afraid to open the Tupperware in our refrigerators. We were *both* guilty of spraying deodorant on dirty socks and throwing them into the dryer on AIR FLUFF. We discovered that while one of us was trying to quick-dry Jockey shorts in the microwave oven (they disappear, all but the waistband) the other one was frantically thawing frozen steaks in the dishwasher (full cycle; no soap). While one of us was stashing trays of dirty dishes in the shower (obviously the oven was already full) the other was stuffing the freezer with pillowcases of mildewed, unironed clothes (long since outgrown).

Neither of us ever knew what costumes our kids were going to wear on Halloween until they went out the door. We each wrote wonderful letters, but neither of us ever mailed them. Our panty hose were eternally run-ridden. We were always locked out, left behind, and overdrawn. (We prayed for the establishment of a new bank called United Security Cash 'n' Run, with a motto of "We rarely balance.")

Finally, stuffed with Eddie's hot dogs, exhausted and emotionally drained, we ended our testimony. By bringing out into the open all the disgusting details of our past, we somehow felt absolutely cleared of it. We decided to forgive ourselves and start over.

2

Why We Used to Be the Way We Were

*W*e planned to meet every week at Eddie's Villa del Weenie to map our strategy. Admitting how we used to be was one thing; understanding *why* we were "The Way We Were" (we've gotta get that name and address) took us a week. Were we lazy? Were we stupid? Were we spoiled? Why were we failures at our *chosen* profession? We loved our homes and families. We realized that being a stay-at-home mom carried with it awesome responsibilities. After all, weren't we supposed to create homes with an atmosphere of joy, peace, beauty, and order? We were responsible for producing the future citizens of the United States of America. We each had a plaque in our kitchen that read:

If there is righteousness in the heart,
There will be beauty in the character.
If there is beauty in the character,

There will be harmony in the home.
If there is harmony in the home,
There will be order in the nation.
If there is order in the nation,
There will be peace on earth.

We agreed with those words, even though they did have peanut butter smeared on them.

We decided to make a list of our reasons and extenuating circumstances (excuses) for being sidetracked. After we had made the list, we numbered each reason. From that day on, whenever we failed, we would just refer to the number of the excuse, instead of wasting time by reciting the whole thing. Some days our extenuating circumstances would be 7 through 155. No matter how appropriate the excuse, we suddenly realized that making excuses did nothing to get us out of the mess. So *we stopped making them.*

Phyllis Diller must hate housework because she once said that she always keeps a desk drawer full of "get well" cards, in case someone comes over unexpectedly and catches her still in her pajamas at two in the afternoon. She quickly whips out all the cards and spreads them across the mantel. Then she answers the door and says, feebly, "Oh, hi, you'll have to excuse the mess. As you can see, I'm just recovering from a really bad bout with the flu!"

With excuse-making behind us forever, the next obstacle was obvious—we had lousy habits. We would never pick up anything; instead we'd pass up the same article over and over until finally we had memorized where everything was. That was the only way we could keep from

TABLE OF EXCUSES

1. I don't have enough energy.
2. It's too hot.
3. It's too cold.
4. I'm not in the mood.
5. I've got too many kids.
6. My husband is working swing.
7. I've got cramps.
8. My house is too small.
9. My house is too big.
10. We just moved in (two years ago).
11. We just got back from vacation.
12. I don't have enough time.
13. We're remodeling.
14. Nobody cooperates with me.
15. I'd rather play solitaire.
16. I don't want to do it.
17. I'm too intelligent for such remedial work.
18. My mother didn't teach me.
19. I hate housework.
20. Nobody appreciates it anyway.
21. Creative people are messy.
22. I'm pregnant.
23. I'll start tomorrow.
24. I was up all night with the baby.
25. It's the flu season.
26. . . . .
27. . . . .
28. . . . .

—

killing ourselves, going down the hall at night to get a drink. We were an anthropologist's dream, leaving a perfect trail behind us of everything we'd ever done. The evidence of our every activity was there for all to see.

Habits are automatic actions that take no conscious thought. When we walk, we don't have to think about it; we just do it. Good habits are silent helpers. Organized people have established a force of good habits.

There's a story told about a baby elephant who was tethered to a pole by a steel ankle bracelet and a heavy six-foot chain. When the animal was fully grown, his trainer removed the chain, leaving only the ankle bracelet. The elephant never ventured beyond the six-foot radius that previously had confined him; he was bound only by a habit.

Dr. Maxwell Maltz, author of *Psychocybernetics,* wrote that, regardless of a person's age or sex, it takes twenty-one days to change a habit. Through his work as a plastic surgeon Maltz discovered that, in virtually every case involving amputation, it took his patient twenty-one days to lose the ghost-image of the missing limb. Maltz began to study the correlation between the human mind and the twenty-one-day period. He proved scientifically that an idea must be repeated for twenty-one consecutive days before it becomes permanently fixed in the subconscious.

We set to work establishing new habits. We posted a list on the refrigerator as a reminder of our goals. The twenty-one-day theory is true. After three weeks of picking things up instead of passing them up, it hurt our brains to step over a Lego.

ESTABLISH THESE HABITS

Put things where they belong when you are through with them.

Set the standard for orderliness yourself.

Never leave the room before closing closets, cupboard doors, and drawers.

Pick it up, don't pass it up; then put it away!

When you fix anything to eat, put away everything you used before you sit down to eat.

Dress, hair, and makeup before ANYTHING.

Never leave the house before you've done all the everyday duties in the card file.

Check the next day's cards the night before.

Finish what you start.

Aside from making excuses and having lousy habits, we felt compelled to say "Yes" to every request. "Yes, I'll sew eight butterfly costumes for the Spring Pageant" (even though *my* kids are going to be the weeds). "Sure, I'll teach forty-nine Cub Scouts needlepoint." "OK, I'll picket the massage parlor from ten to two if you're sure there won't be TV coverage!"

We were afraid to say no for fear of being stamped uncooperative. We needed the approval of others, and saying yes was one way to get it. In that first week of soul-searching, we made the astonishing discovery that we needed to give others the opportunity to be praised. By leaving some of the work for others, we also were leaving them a chance to get the credit. So, charitably, we posted a sign by our phones that read, in capital letters, "SAY

NO!" and from that day on, we rejoiced in our freedom to decline.

At that point in our reformation we began to realize the value of establishing priorities. In the past we had easily been distracted from the task at hand by other members of our families, or sidetracked by our whims, our moods, or outside circumstances. We had every good intention, and *started* elaborate projects with gusto, yet we never completed anything. Scattered around our homes were the remains of half-finished creations: a baby sweater with no sleeves, a blouse with no buttonholes, a thousand quilt patches, and a canvas painted with nothing but sky.

We had always assumed we were sidetracked because of a lack of self-discipline. We thought that self-discipline meant being on time, passing up fattening desserts, controlling our intake of salt—all those things that were hard for us. What we hadn't realized was that the things that came easily were evidence of the self-discipline that we possessed but had not recognized and appreciated. There were areas in our lives where we both displayed phenomenal self-discipline, but in others we had totally failed to use it. We could be put on "hold" indefinitely; we could wait for hours to be served in a restaurant; and, when we answered the phone, even if we were in the middle of a family crisis or if the call came in the middle of the night, we felt we had an obligation to the caller to answer "happy." At times such as these we would be calling on self-discipline, all right—using the "self" to decide for ourselves the order of importance of the things we had to do, using the "discipline" to be firm enough to stick to our decision regardless of who or what was pressuring us to do something else.

In examining our faults, we never lost sight of the good we recognized in each other. We were thankful for the gift of flexibility. We both enjoy easygoing natures. We love life! We love people! We are never bored because everything sounds good to us: a trip to the store, a walk on the beach, a ride to the garbage dump. We embrace the gifts life has given us. We appreciate and celebrate them daily. We salute that goodness in everyone we meet. After all of our self-evaluation, the bottom line had to be saluting the goodness within ourselves.

We had stopped making excuses, and we were aware of our habits. Now we focused our attention on the good ideas we had about ourselves. This time we weren't searching for compliments. This time we weren't affected by criticism. This time we wanted to be organized for *US!* We called it "enlightened selfishness" because we knew it was for the good of all concerned.

In all of our futile attempts to get organized in the past, our motive had been to impress someone else. How ridiculous! We were forever on the defensive, trying to dodge criticism and justify our positions. We were always playing the overworked role.

"Go ahead, pile one more job on me; I can take it." (I won't get it done, but I can take it.)

"Someday I'll drop dead from fatigue and you'll have to hire somebody to take my place."

We fantasized about how our families would feel if they found us one morning, slumped over the clothes hamper in the corner of the utility room, exhausted from doing laundry all night. We had the feeling that even if we were declared clinically dead, our families would manage to find a way to prop us up against the stove, with a pancake turner lashed to one hand and a pound of bacon to the other. Everything seemed so futile in those martyr days. We thought, "Sure, we could be two of those perfectly organized women if we wanted to, but did our families realize what we'd lose: our creativity, our spontaneity, our laughter, and our vitality?" We saw ourselves moving from job to job with no emotion, stripped of our zest for living:

"Daddy, why is Mom so sad?"
"Don't bother her, dear. She's organized—that's the price we must pay to have hot meals and clean clothes."

No more would we consider our child's request to tell him a story or read him a book as the most honored invitation we had ever received. HA! "Move aside, lad, I'm cleaning the groove in the patio door."

Is THAT what they wanted? NEVER! Of course they didn't want us to change. In a surge of self-righteous indignation, we succumbed to that all-too-frequent wave of poetic creativity and placed the following want ad:

WANTED: MOTHERS

We are hiring mothers, and we need them right
away!
You must be filled with peace and joy and vow
that you will stay.
You must appreciate a flower when it's given
without a stem,
Marvel at an ugly rock as if it were a gem.
You must possess a wealth of love, be wise,
controlled, alert.
Have management ability and make a good dessert.
Expertise in finance and a flair for decorating.
Knowledge of psychiatry and Band-Aid applicating.
Willing to accommodate pet relationships.
Detective skills in cases like the missing chocolate
chips.
Qualified and competent in diplomatic circles,
adolescent counseling, in short—performing
miracles.
Adept in kissing bruises and using rocking chairs,
Capable of handling community affairs.
A magician in the kitchen with a pound of
hamburger.
An ability to touch a cheek and know its
temperature.
If you think that you can qualify and you've had
experience
And you understand completely that you make the
difference
Between a world that's filled with fear and a world
that's full of joy,
Call us now, we want you to be in our employ.

3

One Foot Out of the Pigpen

*I*n all our weekly planning sessions at the Villa del Weenie, we never got to know Eddie. We occasionally saw a hot dog fly through the air from the kitchen, and assumed he was back there. It was obvious he was a baseball fan, with all the graffiti on the walls. Several wallet-sized photos, blown up beyond recognition to the size of a cinema screen, adorned the Villa. Eddie *claimed* the pictures were of Hall of Famers, but it could never be proved. The primary subject of each photograph was the familiar figure of a man in the background with a tray of hot dogs strapped to himself (at the photographic expense, in most cases, of just a close-up of some catcher's armpit).

In 1965 Eddie had married Torteena, whose dream was to open a Mexican restaurant, and the rest ... history. It was a shame that they never had any kids. They obviously enjoyed them, or they wouldn't have gone to the ex-

---

pense of having so much entertainment geared to children. Instead of printing the "kiddie menu" on punch-out masks, theirs came printed on the inside of complete costumes. Our kids especially liked the bull costume, which vaguely resembled the enormous mechanical bull that moved on a track, passing each table every ten minutes. (It made six revolutions an hour, dragging a salad bar.) With our children mesmerized by the revolving bull, we were free to continue our journey from a pigpen to paradise.

In gathering the wealth of knowledge from all the books we'd read on time management and home economics, we understood why they hadn't changed us. The authors had impressive credentials, but somehow we didn't relate to their methods and techniques. They didn't understand our sidetracked natures, and we didn't understand their effortless ability to manage. We concluded that a person is either BORN ORGANIZED or not, and we obviously were *not!* We called the person who is born organized a B.O.

Over the years we had asked our friend Nancy, who is a B.O., "How do you do it? The scenery on your telephone-book cover is unblemished by phone numbers scribbled in haste.

"When you eat corn on the cob, you shirr it off in neat rows.

"You clip coupons and USE them!

"You have spare bags and a belt for your vacuum cleaner.

"You started those tomato plants from seed, and you catalogue and alphabetize *everything!*

"You apologize for messes that don't exist.

"You don't have to iron your permanent press.

"You use your TIMED BAKE button.

"When it says, 'DON'T BLEACH,' you *don't*.

"You have a hanky in your purse.

"You count calories *honestly*.

"Open-heart surgery could be performed on the floor of any room in your house.

"You rotate your leftovers and have spare car keys tucked away securely in a magnetic container under the car.

"You have film in your camera, batteries in your flashlight, and you were BORN ON YOUR DUE DATE!.... How do you do it?"

Nancy's reply was always the same: "Oh, I don't know, I just do it!"

Finally we discovered that the missing ingredient in most of the books, written by people who were born organized, was UNDERSTANDING. The B.O. didn't understand how we could desire order but live in chaos. That contradiction is what causes frustration and guilt. We lacked a starting place and direction. A person with energy and desire but no DIRECTION is like lightning in a thunderstorm—devastating. We needed to channel our energy in one direction and not jump all over the house, creating more confusion.

Nancy found our homes were always good for a laugh and liked to drop in before ten to get her day started on a humorous note. She enjoyed our fun-loving attitudes and found it remarkable that we could laugh in the face of such chaos. We entertained her regularly, and she delighted in watching us in our endless creative endeavors.

One morning in June, at about nine-fifteen (after all of her housework was finished and she'd put up six batches

of jam from strawberries she'd picked earlier), Nancy dropped by on her way to Bible study. On this particular summer morning she found us together, embarking on a new project. We had an idea to start a business, Drop Your Tot & Shop. Our ideas were always clothed in extravagant promotions and campaigns. We had dreams of seeing lines of toddlers begging their mothers to leave them in our loving care: "Mommy, Tony don't wanna go to Ducky World. Tony wanna play over there."

We could never get our dreams off the ground because disorganization affects every area of a person's life (even her dreams). Nancy pulled us away from our wonderful fantasies and into the reality of a messy kitchen, with a request for another cup of tea.

"Nancy, HELP! We need advice. We're going down for the third time. Isn't there something concrete you can tell us?"

She took a deep breath as she searched her mind for just the right morsel of information. We sat motionless on the edge of our chairs, waiting for something she might say that would solve our problems. There was a silence that seemed to last an eternity, and then she spoke. "When you fix a cup of tea . . ."

"Yeah . . ."

"Do you use ONE bag for ONE cup?"

"Yeah," we answered simultaneously. (We thought she was going to give us some wonderful and exotic tea recipe.)

She continued, "If you use ONE bag for ONE cup, then why are all of those tea bags lined up over there on the counter?" Our heads turned in unison, following her pointing finger to the row of soggy tea bags.

"Oh, yeah . . ." We listened intently.

—

"See," she continued, "what you do is make the cup of tea and then you THROW THE BAG AWAY!"

"Oh, yeah?"

We were totally taken by the wisdom flowing from her lips. Our lives were filled with that kind of unconscious clutter.

Nancy's advice was all we could handle at that time, and we felt indebted, much to her amazement.

A Sidetracked Home Executive (S.H.E.) is a special kind of person. A S.H.E. can never be one of the born-organized people, but a S.H.E. can learn much from her organized friends. A S.H.E. must realize her self-discipline is not missing; it is just dormant. What she does lack is direction. She suffers from what we call the IGAD disease (I've Got All Day). She has very little awareness of time, and neither had we:

"Eeegad! It's four-thirty and I'm not dressed yet. What do you mean, 'What's for dinner?'?"

With no time card to punch, no deadlines to meet, no foreman to guide and oversee our progress, hours would disappear into days, days into weeks, and months into years. Every New Year's Eve our main resolution was to GET ORGANIZED! But by February 20 (as we were taking down the Christmas tree) we would realize we'd failed again.

It had only been seven days since our decision to change, but already there was a remarkable improvement in our attitude. In releasing all ties to the past, we carried forth only the understanding we had gained from its experience.

William James, a famous Harvard philosopher and

teacher, said, "The greatest discovery in my generation is that by changing your attitude you can change your circumstances." Any successful person knows that a change in thinking is the first step to victory. It all starts from within. Why, then, do we often look for change outside of ourselves? Why do we try to change our *circumstances* in hopes that it will change our attitudes? We get sidetracked. We just keep forgetting to look within for wisdom. We gradually learn through experience that all of our searching, striving, acting, and reacting has been in vain. What we thought would make us happy didn't, like a child who eagerly awaits Christmas with all its surprises and finds that the newness wears off. When do we ever grow up? Can we learn from those who have been rich and famous and yet lead lives of quiet desperation? In stilling that loud voice that often tries to convince us that we cannot succeed, we begin to feel the gentle nudging of a far more powerful, positive voice. We must let *that* voice guide us.

We changed our attitudes immensely in those first few weeks. Our new outlook helped us to see what our next step should be: OUR APPEARANCE! We looked awful! In all the photos of special get-togethers, we were two typically dumpy housewives.

If we were thinking of ourselves as professional homemakers, we certainly didn't dress for the role. What executive would go to work in sweatpants and sneakers? No self-respecting businesswoman would go to her office devoid of makeup and with a hairdo that had dried on the vine. We made a rule that we would get up one half hour before the main part of the family. (Inevitably when we say this rule in a get-organized workshop, someone always asks us how to cope with a radically early riser.

Our answer is always the same: "If some turkey gets up at five A.M., he's on his own. You're only required to get up a half hour before the mainstream of the family.") We used that half hour to take a shower, fix our hair, put on makeup (we decided if we wore makeup out, we should wear it at home), and dress. Incidentally, getting dressed means all the way down to SHOES. If you wear slippers, that tells your mind, "Oh, we're going to lounge around today." In those early days our toddlers weren't used to seeing us dressed before lunchtime and clung to us. "Go bye-bye, Mama?"

A few words of caution: When you start fixing yourself up in the morning, be prepared to lose forty-five minutes. Our husbands would grab us and . . .

Since it is a rule to get up earlier, we tell all of our students to do it. One woman returned to class with this story: "I got up like you said we have to do, and I showered, shampooed my hair, and put my makeup on. I felt wonderful! I went to wake up my teenage son, and he said, 'Aw, Mom, you slept in your clothes!'"

Actually, it was even a bit of a shock to us to pass ourselves in a mirror and catch a glimpse of a stranger in our house. We began complimenting ourselves for looking so nice. "Oh, now don't you look pretty!" We felt a little strange at first, giving compliments to an image in the mirror, but we decided we needed some positive strokes. Was it egotistical to tell ourselves how well we were doing? NO! We decided that, if egotistical people would take some time to tell themselves they were "all right," maybe they wouldn't have to tell everybody else.

We analyzed that, if we looked as if we just might have a few good ideas, we would improve our image as pro-

fessional home executives. We didn't run out and buy white uniforms, white work shoes, support hose, and hairnets. (As a joke in one of our workshops, we told everyone to do just that. The next week a student, who obviously had taken us seriously, said, "I can't quite get used to this white hairnet, but I LOVE my new work shoes!" We gave each other quick glances. Right after class we bought work shoes—not the steel-toed industrial kind, but good sturdy tie shoes. We found they really helped our stamina, and now we honestly—no joke—recommend them.)

Getting up earlier is not easy for people like us, but we found that whenever we didn't follow our first rule to get up early, we didn't have time for ourselves. There were too many other things to be done for the family in the morning rush. If we got up early but stayed in our nightgowns, our beds worked like high-powered magnets, pulling us right back under the covers.

MAKE BED. That was our second rule, and if someone was in the bed, that was no excuse. That *go back to bed* sleep isn't restful anyway. It usually brings with it Alice-in-Wonderland dreams, moving in and out of the reality of *Sesame Street* on TV; visions of Big Bird falling into a great bowl of oatmeal, and then back to sleep; cries from hungry children, interrupted by the sound of running water . . . NO THANKS! Getting up early was hard but worth the sacrifice.

When we met that second week at Eddie's, we were gorgeous! Our attitudes were superb; our enthusiasm for what was happening in our homes gave us new life! We saw that we could never go back to our old patterns. That's when Torteena (she was our waitress) noticed the change. "What is happening to you two? You both look fantastic! What is your secret?" At that point all we could say was, "We changed our minds and we get up half an hour earlier." (Not very impressive.)

We moved into the next phase of our metamorphosis. We questioned where to go from here. There was a lot left to do, but we knew we'd come a long way.

What next? Should we get our kids involved? We realized that we weren't quite ready to do much delegating and teaching at this point. We had to be examples first. We must set the standard for orderliness ourselves and then guide the little ones, ranging from one to twelve years old. What next, then? We were very cautious about getting sidetracked again. We knew that one brilliant idea could send us off to Discount Hack-n-Hang-It (a wallpaper store) or Fran's Fabric Island. We were wise.

We felt an overwhelming desire to tell the world about how we were changing.

An idea told before its time is never as effective as it is when it is ready to be born. We decided not to tell our friends, but it soon became quite evident that one of us had goofed up by telling her husband. Husband "A" wasn't told. Husband "B" was told:

"I'm taking a class on how to get organized."

"Is that right? Where?"

"Down at Eddie's Villa del Weenie."

"Really?"

"Really!"

"How long have you been going?"

"Two weeks."

"Is it a big class?"

"No, actually it's quite small."

"How many students?"

"Two."

"Two? Who teaches it?"

"Well, I teach it one week and Sissy teaches it the next."

"Oh, you guys, that's just another excuse to go have lunch. You ought to write a book on excuses!"

Husband "A," who was left in the dark, said in the fourth week of our meetings, "What's going on here? You look wonderful, you smell good, and the house is immaculate. I thought you would have fallen off this *kick* by now. You're either pregnant or having an affair."

"Neither. I AM ORGANIZED!"

It's better to keep your decision to change under your bonnet. There are several reasons for this. When you make the decision to keep your mouth shut, you build up energy. (Think back on how hard it is to *guard* a secret!) Keep it inside until it has time to grow with you. Don't let it be born prematurely. It will help create a burning desire to succeed. Wait until someone asks, "What's happened to you?" and *then* blast your face off. Another reason for keeping quiet is the negative response that so many well-doers have for you. "Organized—that's a good one." "Oh, sure, Marge, you're getting organized? Remember the last time you tried and failed?"

Don't give anyone the power to cause you to doubt your ability to do ANYTHING. One of the best ways to do that is not to tell what you are up to.

We surrounded ourselves only with positives. We read all the inspirational writings we could get our hands on. We spent less time talking on the phone to friends who wanted to talk about their scars. We watched what we were saying, which might be a key to some negative thinking, and we quit watching soap operas. In the midst of change, we could not afford to concern ourselves with negative people. The soaps are full of pathetic souls just getting out of trouble, just getting into trouble, and in general, this spells trouble for you. Rule three was CUT OUT THE SOAPS.

In analyzing a S.H.E., we mentioned that she lacks direction. With us the problem was finding a direction that wouldn't box us in. The list-making way of getting organized was definitely out. We used to make grand and glorious lists, with priorities in red ink and lesser jobs in graduating colors of the rainbow. With a list of ten things to do on Monday, we'd do three, carry over seven, Tuesday add ten, do three, carry over fourteen, do two, and by Friday we'd have a list of 16,000 things and the baby would eat the list! NO MORE LISTS.

Out of a problem that had mastered us, we found the answer: a system that changed our lives and has helped hundreds of women like us.

We Change Lives with 3×5's

*T*he system works; we KNOW it does. But to convince any doubting S.H.E.s about its effectiveness, we take you now to the home of Waynette Crystal, four months after her disastrous meeting (from under the tent in the hall) with her husband's boss.

WAYNETTE'S STORY

Ten A.M. Barney had to come home from work to change clothes for a special assignment. He brought his boss—with the Darth Vader voice—home with him. Since we were remodeling then, we had taken down all the doors in the house for refinishing, including the closet and cupboard doors. My husband's always bringing people in through the back door. As Barney escorted his boss in and down the hall, I saw the man look in every bathroom and bedroom.

—

Using the system, I'd already made sure the house was immaculate that morning, including the open cupboards. My hair was combed, makeup on, and I was gorgeous. The kids were playing contentedly as in one of the *Brady Bunch* shows. It was my baking day, and the house was filled with the aroma of freshly baked pie.

Barney went to change his clothes, and I took his boss into the living room. He sat down, and I could see he was looking around.

"Would you like a cup of coffee and a piece of cherry pie?" I asked casually. For a fleeting moment I thought, "Who said that?" I remembered the last time he was here, when I was buried in Friskies and chocolate chips in the tent with the kids.

He said he would love a piece of pie and a cup of coffee. So I went to the kitchen and thought, "I can't believe I've actually got a REAL piece of pie here. A year ago I would have been lucky to find the COFFEE!"

I put the pie and coffee on a darling little tray and took it to the living room. Barney's boss said, "Mrs. Shedlester, I . . . I just have to say something. It's ten o'clock in the morning, and this place is absolutely spotless, and you've got three little kids here, and they haven't made a sound. They're just playing together so cute."

Then came the magic words: "How do you do it?" he asked. "How can you have pie and coffee ready this early? HOW DO YOU POSSIBLY DO IT?"

"Oh, I don't know," I said modestly. "I just . . . do it, I guess." I turned and moved gracefully into the kitchen, a bit like Audrey Hepburn. As soon as I was out of his sight I collapsed on the counter in sheer ecstasy! Then do you know what I did? I took a pink 3×5 card and wrote

down, "Mrs. Shedlester, I just have to say something....
How do you possibly do it?"

I wrote his whole speech on the card, dated it, and filed
it in a divider called Compliments, in the little box that
holds our system. I wanted more of those experiences,
and the effort was worth it. How exciting to change SO
much SO fast. (I learned several months later that Barney's
boss thought Barney had remarried.)

Supplies you'll need for the system: a 3×5 file box; 25
yellow, 25 blue, and 25 pink 3×5 cards; 100 white 3×5
cards; 4 or more blank dividers; 12 dividers labeled
January through December; 31 dividers numbered 1
through 31; 26 dividers labeled with the letters of the
alphabet; and a small calendar showing the year at a
glance. Try your checkbook register. You can cut out the
calendar and cut it to fit inside your file box. Tape it to
the inside of the lid.

Study the Activity List (see Appendix, pp. 135–162).
Use these pages as work sheets. Unless you borrowed
this book, WRITE IN IT! The Activity List is the basis of
our system, the tool for organizing your house and your
life. Make additions or deletions as necessary; it should
reflect your lifestyle.

Every room of the house is on the Activity List. Any
rooms in your house that are not found on our list will
have to be added, such as a library, sewing room, barn,
etc.

Decide how many of the list's activities apply to you
and your family and how often they should be done: daily, every other day, weekly, every other week, monthly,
every other month, seasonally, twice a year, or yearly.
Put down how often you *want* to do it, NOT HOW OF-

—

TEN YOU'RE DOING IT NOW. We know you're not doing it now, or you wouldn't be reading this book. The idea is to plan to do a job often enough so the house is as clean as if you had a cleaning person come in.

Then put a time estimate on each activity—how long you think it takes to finish a job. For instance, we thought it took twenty minutes to vacuum the living room. But after we timed it we found it took only about seven minutes. We want you to be aware of time because losing track of time is a typical problem for S.H.E.s.

As you personalize your own Activity List you'll include: what has to be done, how often it should be done, how long it will take, whether you can delegate it to your husband, children, or outside help (in a later chapter we'll tell you how to get your family involved in the system), and whether it's a Mini-Job.

A Mini-Job is any project, regardless of how frequently it should be done, that takes ten minutes or less to complete. We emphasize Mini-Jobs on the Activity List because, if you're sidetracked by nature, you can go through the day unaware of what you could have done with small blocks of time.

Note on the Activity List all the Mini-Jobs that can be done while you're talking on the phone or waiting for appointments. Put this list by your phone and make the ringing of the telephone a subconscious alarm for you to find a Mini-Job to do while talking. Your first mini-task could be grabbing a drawer and cleaning it out during your next phone conversation. Always keep a couple of thank-you notes, complete with envelopes and stamps, in your purse, for those times when you find yourself waiting for the dentist, doctor or Oil Can Henry.

When you have adapted our Activity List to your

FILL THE SPACES

Select a large box, and place in it as many
cannonballs as it will hold, and it is,
after a fashion, full; but it will hold more
if smaller matters be found. Bring a quantity
of marbles; very many of these may be
packed in the spaces between the larger globes;
the box is now full, but still only in a sense;
it will contain more yet. There are spaces in
abundance, into which you may shake a consid-
    erable
quantity of small shot, and now the
chest is filled beyond all question; but yet
there is room. You cannot put in another shot
or marble, much less another ball; but you will
find that several pounds of sand will slide
down between the larger materials, and, even
then between the granules of sand, if you
empty yonder jug, there will be space for all
the water, and for the same quantity several
times repeated. Where there is no space for the
    great, there may be room for the little;
where the little cannot enter, the less can
make its way: and where the less is shut
out, the least of all may find ample
room. So where time is, as we say, fully occupied,
there must be stray moments, occasional intervals,
and bits of time which might hold a
vast amount of little usefulness in the course
of months and years.

—C. H. SPURGEON

needs, your next step is to draw up a Basic Week Plan (see Appendix, p. 155). This is a flexible guide to help you spread your work and activities through the week.

For the full-time homemaker, we suggest setting up a free day for yourself every week, when you can do anything you want: have lunch with friends, read a novel, take a long country walk, learn karate. Your day will be free from housework, elaborate cooking, and errands. It will be your weekly reward for being so well organized that you can afford to take the day off without seeing the house fall apart!

Besides the free day, your Basic Week Plan also should include a moderate cleaning day (two to four hours spent on housework); a quiet day, when you will do things like pay bills, balance the checkbook, clip grocery coupons, write letters, and tie up loose ends; a grocery-shopping day; a heavy-cleaning day (four to six hours of housework); a family day; and Sunday, which is free of cleaning.

The plan can be varied, depending on whether or not you have a job outside your home (see Appendix, p. 155). If you do, you might want to have three moderate-cleaning days (two to four hours of cleaning) instead of one heavy-cleaning and one moderate-cleaning day each week. Housework could be divided into morning (before work) and evening (after work). In that case, jobs should be scheduled around peak-energy times, leaving the easier jobs for low-energy times. You might want to have two Basic Week Plans, one for morning activities and one for evening.

Laundry should be planned according to whether or not that day is an "at home" day or an "outside the home" day. Laundry that needs immediate attention, such as permanent press, would need to be done when you were available to get the clothes out of the dryer quickly. Sheets and towels can be done fast and folded by children as part of their chores. Save the simple laundry for free days and family days, and do the more tedious laundry when time is available.

If you're trying to juggle children, meals, housework, volunteer work, and an outside job, you're going to need help. Open the channels for that help to come to you. Plan for it, expect it, make it a financial priority, but get yourself on the system so that, when the help is available, you'll be ready to accept it. Work the rough spots out until you're in control of the system.

In the beginning celebrate every improvement, no matter how small. Concentrate on the trend. With all of your commitments, you must not allow yourself to be defeated by lack of time. There is enough time to begin, and the next day will take care of itself. Day by day you will find that you are making progress. Don't get into the trap of thinking your neighbor is better off than you are. Everyone has his or her own set of circumstances that can make being organized a real trial. Use the flexibility of the system to get you on the track.

Go over the Basic Week Plans. Take out a white card and make your own plan—no matter how many excuses you can think of for not doing this crucial step. UNLESS YOU START HERE, WITH YOUR BASIC WEEK PLAN, YOU WON'T BE ABLE TO SUCCEED WITH THIS SYSTEM. You don't have to be locked into this plan forever. It's tentative and flexible, but it helps let you know what you're going to do.

Tape the Basic Week Plan below the calendar on the inside of the lid of your card file box.

Before we started the system, friends would call and ask us, "When can you have lunch?" and we'd say, "ANYTIME," and go. We said, "Anytime," to EVERYTHING; we thought we could do everything. But after we set up the system, we started refusing lunch invitations on heavy-cleaning days. We stayed home and cleaned on those days and made time for lunches with friends on other afternoons.

This weekly plan helps you stay away from the ANYTIME routine.

It's neat for us now, not being at the mercy of requests from friends, husband, and children. We established credibility from the beginning, saying firmly, "I'll be available on Wednesday for all the errands you want done. If you'll just give me a list, Wednesday's the day that I'll do it." Then we made sure that on Wednesday we really DID do it!

If a husband got his request in on Thursday, it either waited until the following Wednesday, or he did the errand himself. If the PTA called on Sunday or Monday and asked, "Can you bake two thousand cookies for the open house?" we said, "Gee, if you would've called last week I could have done it, but I can't now. Saturday is my baking day. I just don't have any time to do it now."

You will also realize in the next few weeks that you are experiencing the effects of your OVERBOOKING DAYS. There's no getting out of that promise to make Marsha a spotted owl costume for the endangered species pageant; you've already paid for fifteen consecutive weeks of line-dancing lessons, and you're stuck typing twelve thousand names alphabetically for the statewide skate-a-thon. (After all, at the time you said, "SURE." It was the least you could do for charity.)

—

From now on you'll know your limits. It's also important to remember that in the beginning everything takes longer to clean because you're chiseling, scraping, bulldozing, and pulling yourself out of *years* of accumulated mess. Keep reminding yourself, "I DIDN'T GET INTO THIS MESS OVERNIGHT, AND I'M NOT GOING TO GET OUT OF IT OVERNIGHT."

Next in the system comes the Menu Plan (see Appendix, p. 155), which coincides with the Basic Week Plan. For instance, if Monday is your free day, then on Monday you're going to have leftovers, and it's paper-plate night. You're not going to do a big Martha Stewart dinner unless being a gourmet cook is what you like to do with your free time.

If Tuesday is your moderate-cleaning day, it's chicken for dinner that night. Wednesday is fish. Thursday is a casserole or crock-pot meal, if that's your grocery-shopping day, because you're going to be gone most of the day and will need something you can start early.

Friday is hamburgers, tacos, or spaghetti. Saturday is cook's choice. Sunday is a big dinner—or decide when you want one special meal a week.

We happen to love to cook, but not everyone does, so we wrote a cookbook to help people who struggle in the kitchen. It's called *The Phony Gourmet*. It has seventy-five sneaky, inventive and delicious recipes. Our motto is, "It's not WHAT you do, it's what they THINK you do!"

Take a yellow card and do a Menu Plan.

Now you're ready to transfer the jobs from your Activity List to the cards. Use *yellow* 3×5 cards for all daily and every-other-day housework—*one job to a card.* Use *blue* cards for all weekly and every-other-week jobs. Use *white* cards for monthly and seasonal jobs. Use *pink*

cards for all personal things, the things you love to do, and jobs or errands outside the home, such as going to the bank, post office, etc.

Write the title of the job in the middle of the card. Under it, put "children" or "delegate" in parentheses if someone else could do the job. If you're uncertain of what jobs children can do at specific ages, study the lists on pp. 161-162). Under that, write a description of the job, being as detailed as you want: what articles you use to clean with, what products to use, and any special instructions.

In the card's right-hand corner, put the job's time estimate. If it's a mini-job, write "mini" on the card. In the left-hand corner, write "daily" or "weekly" or whatever the frequency is. It is important to make the cards exactly like the examples we have for you (see pp. 156-157). As you transfer a job from the Activity List to a card, put a check mark by that job on the list to tell you that you have made the card.

When we started, we needed cards for everything because we wouldn't do a job if we didn't have a card for it. But as a job became automatic, we threw its card away. So if you already made your bed without needing to be reminded, you don't need a card for it unless you sometimes want to delegate it to someone else.

We gave our mother, an immaculate housekeeper, a scholarship to our get-organized class for Christmas. During the class we told her, "Now, if it's already a habit, you don't have to have a card for it." Mom had three cards at the end of the class. One was: "Clean the light-diffusing bowls." (That's where all the dead bugs accumulate.)

Next come the 1 through 31 dividers, which will be your rotating monthly "calendar" in your file box. If you stay on the system, you'll always know what day it is by looking in your box. Rotate the numbered dividers until the current date is the first one in the pack. Place the whole set of dividers, 1 through 31, in the front of the file box, starting with today's date. Each night you will rotate the date just ended to the back of the numbers, so that the current date is always in the front of the box.

For example, let's say you're starting the system on the seventh of the month. The divider numbered 7 will be at the front of the box. The rest of the numbers will be filed behind the 7 divider—8 through 31, then the dividers 1 through 6, filed *behind* divider 31, to be rotated day by day through the coming month.

The four blank dividers, months-of-the-year dividers, and the ABCs will be discussed later in this chapter.

After you have transferred ALL jobs onto the cards, you are ready to begin filing. Our first rule is: Always file to the front (the Army does it like that, too) so that your current jobs are in front of the current date.

Make four piles of cards, separated by colors.

File all your personal and outside-the-home (pink) cards in front of their appropriate dates. (Many of them will have specific dates.)

File all your daily (yellow) cards in front of today's date. If you have already completed some of today's jobs, put those cards in front of tomorrow's date. Get in the habit of checking the next day's cards the night before, to see what's coming up. (That last statement is written on your list of habits to establish, and it bears repeating.)

Next file every-other-day (yellow) cards in front of today's date if they haven't been done or the day after tomorrow if you have already completed a job.

From the stack of blue cards, make four separate piles:

1. Weekly mini-jobs.
2. Weekly jobs.
3. Every-other-week mini-jobs.
4. Every-other-week jobs.

Weekly "mini" jobs can be done any day of the week (even on a free day) because they take ten minutes or less. Just be sure not to file any weekly "mini" jobs beyond seven days from the current date. File all blue weekly cards on your moderate-cleaning day or heavy-cleaning day. The only weekly cards that would not go in your moderate- or heavy-cleaning days would be such "quiet" jobs as writing letters, making a grocery list, balancing the checkbook, etc. They would be filed in front of the errand day, the quiet day, or the appropriate day for the particular activity.

The weekly cards have to be spread out within the week. For example, let's say Monday is your free day. The only weekly jobs that you would stick in your Monday file would be mini-jobs that take only ten minutes. Maybe throw in three or four "minis" on your free day. Most of your weekly jobs would go in your moderate-cleaning (Tuesday) or heavy-cleaning day (Friday). Balance the weekly jobs according to the time you have each week—but they can't be spread out any farther than seven days.

Every-other-week mini-jobs also can be filed any day of the next two weeks, but not beyond fourteen days from the current date.

Every-other-week jobs are filed in appropriate days just as you filed the weekly jobs, but aren't to go beyond fourteen days from the current date.

When you have completely filed all the blue cards, move on to the white cards. They, too, must be sorted. Make three separate stacks of white cards:

1. Monthly mini.
2. Monthly.
3. Anything over a month. This stack would include yearly jobs, seasonal jobs, every-other-month jobs, mini or otherwise.

- Monthly mini jobs can be done any day of the month.
- Monthly jobs will be spread out over the eight moderate- and heavy-cleaning days that fall in the next thirty-one days.
- The cards that are left will be filed in the January through December dividers, which are explained in detail at the end of this chapter. Just put those leftover cards aside for now.

We tried desperately at first to do EVERY card in our file at the appointed time. We made it through the "dailies" and "personals" OK, but some of those "weeklies" and "monthlies" were real dogs:

RING RING . . . "Hello?"
"Hi, Sissy, how are you doing?"
"This card file is choking me!"
"Why?"
"Too much to do, not enough time, too hot, too tired—excuses sixteen through forty-three, you know!"
"What card are you supposed to do?"

"Wash and wax the family-room floor, but I just *can't* do it."

"Could you just do part of it? Suppose you only had to wash and wax four tiles . . . just four and then you could dump out the bucket, put away the mop, and go lie in the sun. . . . Let's get all our work done so you can go and play. Listen to what I wrote, this'll inspire you:

SUMMER POEM

Summertime is sippin' lemonade and feelin' cool.
Summertime's a jackknife off the board into the pool.
Summertime's a hammock strung between two big oak
  trees.
Lookin' at the sky of blue, listenin' to the breeze.
Summertime is baseball games and reruns on TV.
Summertime is mowin' lawns and steppin' on a bee.
Summertime is picnics in the park with lots of ants.
Summertime is bare feet and a hole torn in your pants.
Summertime is butterflies and daisies growing wild.
In summertime it's easy to enjoy life like a child.
Summertime is sunscreen and soaking in the sun.
Roll over on your tummy . . . when your back is done.
Summertime's a special time to share your light with all.
So why not call a friend before it turns to fall!

"Makes me want to go to Battle Ground Lake!"

"Let's go!"

"I can't with this stupid white card screaming at me to WASH AND WAX THE FAMILY-ROOM FLOOR!"

"Well, hurry up, then, and get started. I'll guarantee that if you get a nice bucket of hot sudsy water and tell yourself you only have to do *four* tiles, you won't be *able* to quit until the job is done! Go on, now. Hang up and call me when you're finished."

FOUR MINUTES LATER

Ring. Ring . . .

"I'm finished! I did the four tiles you *made* me do and then I dumped my nice bucket of sudsy water and tore up the little white card!"

"YOU DID WHAT? You actually TORE UP a 3×5? How could you?"

"I didn't, really. . . . I just wanted to scare you, but there's no way I'm going to do that floor today. This is supposed to be my moderate-cleaning day, and I've already done four hours' worth of cards. There's a limit! I'm through for today."

"OK, so you didn't do the job. Where are you going to file the card?"

"Should I put it in front of tomorrow's date?"

"No, tomorrow's your free day."

"Day after tomorrow?"

"That's your grocery day."

"Okay, then, how about putting it in my next heavy-cleaning day this week? . . . No, I can't. It's already *full* of cards."

"Okay, it's supposed to be done once a month, and if you had actually done the job, you'd file it a month from today on a moderate-cleaning day, right?"

"Right."

"I think you should file it as though you had done it."

[GASP!] "What are you SAYING? Skip it for an entire month? How *could* I?"

"What do you mean, 'HOW COULD I?'? You haven't done that floor for six years. What's another month?"

"Yeah?"

"FILE IT AND FORGET IT. It's not like you're neglecting it because four weeks from now it'll come up again. You're just rescheduling it."

"YEAH! And in a month from now things will be just that much further ahead."

We rejoiced in finding a way of preventing jobs from piling up beyond our ability to cope. Now we were free to skip weekly and monthly jobs when necessary without guilt. FILE IT AND FORGET IT was our new motto. It gave the system flexibility and freedom. Unfortunately, in the ensuing weeks we found ourselves skipping the same cards over and over, not necessarily because we were short of time but because we found the job distasteful. Sooner or later, if we wanted to enjoy the beauty of a polished family-room floor, we'd have to do the card. We had to put some restraints on our newfound freedom.

At the bottom of each card we wrote the words "LAST DONE *(date)*" in the left-hand corner and "SKIPPED *(date)*" in the right-hand corner (see illustration, p. 157). After a job was completed, we'd pencil in the date and file the card in the next regular date that the job should be done. If the job needed to be skipped, we'd pencil in the date and place an X in the "SKIPPED" blank, and file the card just as if the job had been completed.

We allowed ourselves two skips, but decided that any card having two Xs on it (from being skipped twice) would automatically become a priority and *have* to be completed the next time it appeared in the card file. Once the job was finished, the Xs would be erased and the date penciled in as "LAST DONE."

An X is fine for skipping a single job, you say, but what

—

about skipping a whole DAY? What if your friend from South Africa comes to town and calls you to have lunch, and it's your heavy-cleaning day? Are you going to tell her, "I'm so very sorry, dahling, but my executive house-cleaning system does not permit lunchtime interruptions on Fridays. Perhaps the next time you're on this continent . . .?" Do we answer the phone, "Heavy-cleaning day"?

We don't want you to get so rigid that you turn into a mechanical person who can't switch your schedule. Definitely put PEOPLE before this system. What you do is take all the cards from your heavy-cleaning day and—don't X them—exchange them with your free day for that week. Just remember to go back to your regular week's plan the following week.

When you go on vacation for a week or the pears in the backyard are ripe and the canning will take a week, just skip every card that is in that week (except anything that could pile up, such as dishes and laundry) and file all the cards for when you're back to normal.

Finally, you're ready to organize the January through December dividers.

Take the stack of white cards (every-other-month, seasonal, yearly, etc.) that we left you with earlier, and file them in front of the appropriate month you wish to accomplish the job in. Example: If this is July, file all every-other-month cards in front of September. Seasonal jobs such as cleaning gutters, fertilizing the lawn, etc., will be filed in front of the right month.

Now take twelve blank white cards, one for each month, and transfer all birthdays, anniversaries, and other special dates from your calendars, address books, and crumpled paper-towel notes onto the cards. List all January dates on ONE card (see illustration, p. 157), and do the same for the other eleven months. File each white card in front of the appropriate January through December divider.

You also will file future dates, such as dinner parties, dental appointments, etc., in front of the corresponding month's divider. But write those onetime, temporary dates on 3×5 scratch paper, not on the cards. Once you've used the "dental app't." note, you can remove it from the file and throw it away.

Now take out a white 3×5 card and write the words "CHECK DATES to REMEMBER" (see illustration, p. 158). File that card in front of the twenty-fifth (daily numbered divider). That card will ALWAYS remain there as a tickler to remind you to check the next month's cards.

On the twenty-fifth of each month, you will pull out all the cards in the following month's divider and file them in front of the appropriate days. It's a good idea to file the single birthday/special-occasion card in front of your first shopping day, so you can buy all that month's gifts and cards at one time. Then you can rotate the birthday/special-occasion card throughout the month as a reminder to mail in time or, celebrate the event. One time we totally forgot Halloween. After you celebrate the last special occasion for that month, refile the birthday/special-occasion card in front of the appropriate monthly divider—all ready for next year!

Other cards to file in the monthly-divider section include seasonal jobs, appointments made far in advance, dates of conventions or shows you'll attend, and every-other-month jobs.

You'll have a problem with the next step if you have a

strong, sentimental attachment to your address book. We want you to transfer all names, addresses (including Zip codes), phone numbers, e-mail addresses, FAX, and mobile numbers from your book to white cards. Your new system of address cards will give you space to write special notations, such as names of children, hobbies, collections, etc. (see illustration, p. 158).

It's so nice to have personalized information about your friends. For example, we have a friend in California named Gisela. Whenever we'd start to write to her, the same question would always come up. Is it G-I-S-E-L-L-A or G-E-E-S-I-L-A? The choice was then to chance spelling her name incorrectly (an unthinkable); to write, "Hi, Friend" (another unthinkable); or not to write at all. Needless to say, Gisela never heard from us! After we ditched our dog-eared address books and kept everyone's name in our card file, we were gradually able to come up with the proper spelling of people we loved: "Dear Gisela: How are the kids, Torsten and Elise? Say Hi to Tom. . . ." It felt so good to spell people's names right.

It's a joy, too, to keep track of "new arrivals." Such an important event as a new baby merits your remembering. When you receive a birth announcement from a couple, add the baby's birth date, name, weight, etc. (see Illustration, p. 158). Think how surprised you'd be to receive a card from a friend on your child's birthday.

Our streamlined information turned out to be a real time-saver, too. We figured we wasted at least sixty hours a year, first looking for the phone book and then trying to read the number off the scenery on the cover. Now whenever we get a number from directory assistance, we make out a card so we don't have to waste time and money calling again. Also, unlisted phone numbers of friends should be transferred to cards.

In addition to cards for people you love, make out separate cards for your doctor, dentist, veterinarian, beauty salon, newspaper, credit-card numbers, favorite stores, books you'd like to read, your children's schools, their friends, your car dealer—anyone you might need to call or write to. We have cards for our insurance-policy numbers and bank-account numbers, and cards with early dismissals and school closures that we transfer from the weekly bulletins the kids bring home from school.

File all the cards in front of the appropriate letter in your alphabet-divider section. File early-dismissal and school-closure cards in front of the day they will occur. Such cards as appointments and special occasions should be stood on end in the file box to call your attention to them.

Here are some final rules to remember:

- Never leave the house before you've done all the morning's daily chores in your card file.
- Refile your cards as you complete them.
- Check the next day's cards the night before.

Earlier in this chapter, we mentioned that the purpose of the system is to raise your housekeeping standard to what it would be if you had outside help. There were several times in our lives when our budgets could afford some outside help. However, even with help, the underlying problem remained the same. We were in no position to delegate; consequently, we paid several dollars an hour to have someone come in to hang up everybody's clothes, bail us out from under stacks of dishes, and clear off the mounds of laundry on the couch.

After eighteen months of cleaning our homes from top to bottom totally on our own, we once again have outside help. We decided to hire someone to come in for four hours once a week on our heavy-cleaning day to do a stack of weekly, every-other-week, monthly, or every-other-month cards that have been delegated, by us, for that particular heavy-cleaning day. That, in effect, leaves us free to work on S.H.E. We openly admit that we don't like housework, but that DOES NOT mean we don't love our homes and want them clean. It's OK not to like housework, but it has to be done and you need to realize that you can do it (and be happy). If housework is not what you LOVE to do, you can eventually be relieved of whatever chores you find most time consuming. In our circumstances, to continue without help would have meant we couldn't write this book. We logically delegated specific jobs to free us to do what we felt compelled to do.

What you want to do with the system is free yourself to be able to do the things you were created to do. Let this system help you gain control of your life at home and you will find you can also use it to plan your vacations, further your education, organize your hobbies, and be that special person you were created to be.

RECAPITULATION (OR, "GET BACK IN THE BOX!")

You will always find that there will be times in your life when you completely fall off the track. We are the first to admit we have gotten totally "sidetracked," but we love the implication of that word—it's temporary! Just remember to forgive yourself, don't make excuses, and follow these twenty basic steps:

1. Allow yourself one hour of uninterrupted time.
2. Personalize the Activity List in this book.
3. Transfer ALL jobs to cards—one job per card.
4. Make Basic Week Plan. Paste plan and year's calendar to inside lid of box.
5. Make Menu Plan.
6. Label blank dividers: Storage, Christmas, Family, and Special Projects. We will discuss the first three topics in later chapter. Your Special Projects divider is the place for keeping track of plans for home decorating, writing your novel, mapping your trip to Spain, refinishing the bedroom furniture—any projects that will light up your life. You can have several other dividers in whatever areas interest you: canning, gardening, inspiration, compliments, etc. File the newly labeled dividers between the months and the alphabet in your box.

   By now you're feeling panicky with so many cards. You can be overwhelmed when, for the first time, you actually *see* what it takes to run a home.
7. Put dividers in card file in this order: 1–31, with current date forward; four special dividers; January–December; ABCs; extra cards in back.
8. Make piles of cards according to colors (four piles).

9. Using the calendar and Basic Week Plan, file pink cards first. (Most of them will have specific dates.)

10. File yellow (daily) cards in front of today's date if job has not been done today. Daily jobs already completed can be filed in front of tomorrow's date.

11. File yellow (every-other-day) cards in front of today's date if they haven't been done, or the day after tomorrow if already completed.

12. Sort out blue mini-job cards from the blue pile. Mini-jobs can be filed for any day, even a free day.

13. File all blue (weekly) cards on moderate-cleaning or heavy-cleaning days (except quiet activities, which go on your quiet day).

14. File all blue (every-other-week) cards up to fourteen days from current date.

15. Separate white (monthly and every-other-month) cards into three piles: mini-jobs, monthly, and every other month. File white minis anywhere in the numbers.

16. File all white (monthly) cards in the moderate- or heavy-cleaning days of the month.

17. File every-other-month white cards in the January–December dividers, TWO MONTHS from current month.

18. Transfer birthdays and anniversaries from calendar and file in January–December section.

19. Make out white card "Check dates" and file in front of number 25.

20. Using old address book or phone book, make out cards on loved ones and often-used phone numbers or places of business and file in ABC section.

5

All Dressed Up with a Dirty Neck

*W*hen we were little, we loved to get all dressed up and go out to dinner with Mom and Dad. Quite often we were taken to elegant places so that we could experience and be comfortable in a variety of situations. Mom and Dad believed that on those occasions that we were given the privilege of going with them, it would be not only for enjoyment but also for learning. They wanted our dining experience to go beyond places like Eddie's Villa del Weenie.

Invariably when we'd be on our way to someplace grand, dressed in our finest, the scrutinizing eye of our mother would spot a smudge of dirt on us with radarlike accuracy. Before we knew what hit us, a moistened hanky would appear out of nowhere, and we'd be gone over like a mother cat cleaning her babies.

The lecture was always the same: "You're all dressed up with a *dirty neck!* When will you girls learn that you

---

can't put a pretty dress on over dirt? It would be the same as putting whipped cream on top of a garbage can!"

It was a challenge to see if we could sneak past her, undetected. Somehow she could spot a dirty neck beneath even the best camouflage. Once, in spite of turtleneck sweaters, scarves, beads, chains, makeup, and a fast exit, we were still nabbed at the door and escorted by the "warden" to the bathroom—and given the same lecture.

We never figured out how her mother's instinct could catch us every time until we were raising little "dirty necks" of our own.

We carried the "whipped cream on top of a garbage can" habit into our homes. This method of home management (clean it well enough to fool the company, but keep them confined to the living room) accompanied a list of unwritten rules:

- Guests will keep their coats with them.
- Guests will not loiter in the halls. (Our children were trained to spot and notify us of any visitor loitering near closets.)
- "Out of Order" signs will be placed on all bathrooms except the one we cleaned.

If dinner guests asked if they could help us in the kitchen, we had to decline. We would have died before letting ANYONE look in our oven or the refrigerator. We used to say, "Thank you, but I like to work alone." How could we justify those items in the refrigerator, shriveled beyond recognition, or covered with a fine blue fuzz? Some of the refrigerator residents already had distinct personalities. We both had recurring nightmares of one day opening the refrigerator and having the inhabitants, led by the thirteen-year-old box of Arm & Hammer baking soda, leap out on the kitchen counters, shouting obscenities. They'd march out right in the middle of a dinner party and stage a sit-down around the table centerpiece. Their placards would read:

"BACTERIA ARE BEAUTIFUL!"
"JOBS FOR GERMS!"
"FREE THE FUZZ!"

We feared they had a circuit of underground agents whose ultimate goal was to take over the entire house.

It was no wonder we were having nightmares. We knew that even on those rare occasions when our houses were surface-clean for company, there was a garbage can in every closet, cupboard, and drawer. All the experts in home management (you know, the ones who wrote, "A Place for Everything, and Everything in Its Place!") say you should begin at the beginning, cleaning closets, cupboards, and drawers. We both acknowledged that the experts probably were right. Who could doubt the credibility they'd achieved from years of study and application? But right or wrong, the thought of opening one of our closets and being buried under an avalanche of egg cartons, fake flowers, feathers, and net was more than either of us could bear:

"What are we saving all this junk for?"
"I don't know. . . . Maybe we could make a bunch of corsages for crazy people."

For an instant we were tempted to make some sample

corsages and lay the plans for a distribution campaign, but somehow we found the strength to resist. We were both strongly determined at that point to follow the advice of the pros. When we left each other at Eddie's that day, we were under the impression that we would both begin cleaning closets, cupboards, and drawers. Then, later:

Ring . . . Ring . . .

"Hello?"

"Hi, Sissy. How are you doing on your closets?"

"Great. I've got them *all* started! In fact, I'm cleaning out a drawer while I'm talking. How about you?"

"Well, I've decided not to do mine. I'm cleaning the oven while *I* talk."

"You're kidding. Why?"

"I want some real evidence that I've changed! I want shiny floors and sparkling windows. I want to be proud to open my oven!" ShShShShShShShShShShShSh . . .

"What's that noise?"

"I'm spraying the oven with cleaner. I feel that, once everything is nice and clean, then I can do the closets."

"Maybe you're right. *This* place looks like a cyclone hit it! I started in the hall closet, and I was doing great until I ran into the Monopoly game. I took it into the kids' bedroom and they wanted to know how to play it. We played for just two hours, and I realized, 'Hey, I've gotta get back to that hall closet,' so I started in AGAIN and found the flashlight. It didn't have batteries, so I went to the kitchen to put batteries on the grocery list. I couldn't find a pen, so I went to my purse. The only thing I could find to write with in there was a pencil that needed to be sharpened. The sharpener was back in the kitchen, but I discovered that it was missing its handle. Luckily I remembered that the last time I used it was to sharpen my eyebrow pencil, so I knew the handle would be in my makeup case in the bathroom. I don't know how or why (I guess I felt sweaty), but the next thing I knew, I was taking a shower. . . ."

"Sissy, I don't think we're going to make it. . . . [Cough . . . Cough . . .]"

"What's the matter?"

"This oven cleaner is choking me! I've a notion to write to Ralph Nader and tell him how caustic this product is!"

"What kind do you use?"

"Let me look. . . . [Cough . . . Cough . . .] OH, NO! I just sprayed *Hartz Mountain NO* in a warm oven!"

"What's *Hartz Mountain NO?*"

"It's a repellent to keep animals from wrecking the carpet."

"Well, at least the cat won't go to the bathroom in the oven!"

"[Cough . . . Cough . . .] How soon can you meet me at Eddie's?"

"Again? We just got out of there a few hours ago!"

Fifteen minutes later we were holding an emergency meeting at the Villa, drowning our sorrows in guacamole dip and wondering where we went wrong.

It was now more clear than ever that the experts were right about where to start. (If the cupboards had been organized, the oven never would have been sprayed with pet repellent. . . . It was months before the cats went near the KITCHEN, let alone the oven.) But, obviously, telling us where to start wasn't enough. It was apparent that this was far more complicated than we had at first believed.

—

Our very nature made it impossible for us to STAY in one closet unless we established some rules. We consulted the "how to" books, and they said, "STREAMLINE THE MAIN LIVING AREA."

"HOW?" we asked.

"JUST DO IT!" they said.

We needed an "anti-sidetracking device," something to keep us glued to one spot until we were through. It came in the form of a box marked PUT AWAY. That one innovation was the breakthrough we had been looking for. (More on that later.)

Finally, painfully, we realized that it takes much less time to establish order in a home than it does to look for things and clean up messes caused by disorganization. For us, the chaos spilling onto our heads and into our laps from inside our closets, cupboards, and drawers was causing us monumental frustration. The disorder built because we closed it off. (Out of sight, out of mind.) It's so easy to close doors on problems. Psychiatrists call it repression. We called it all dressed up with a dirty neck.

Starting at the front door, work clockwise around the house, cleaning out and putting in order each closet, cupboard, and drawer in every room, until you work your way back to the front door.

Since you'll also be trying to carry out your card-file system, it will seem as if you're taking a giant step backward because you will need to skip all your weekly and monthly cleaning jobs during this time. You will need to keep up only with daily chores that pile up if left undone, such as laundry and dishes.

Wear a cobbler's apron while you clean closets, cupboards, and drawers. Keep a pen and a 3×5 pad in your apron pocket because, as you clean everything out, you

will discover items you've been needing for years: batteries for the flashlight, lightbulbs, safety pins, drawer organizers, rubber bands, Scotch tape, stamps, etc.

Before you start your first closet, cupboard, or drawer, go to the produce department of your favorite grocery store and take home as many produce boxes (the sturdy ones with the lids) as you can. Mark four of these boxes: GIVE AWAY/SELL, THROW AWAY, PUT AWAY, and STORAGE.

As soon as you've filled it, you will empty the Give Away/Sell box into Goodwill bags or regular boxes (don't waste your produce boxes) to give to charities or friends. It's a good idea to plan a garage sale to turn unwanted items into cash.

The Throw Away box will be emptied often, too—right into your trash cans. You might want to alert your sanitation service to expect extra pickup that week.

When filling those boxes to give away, sell, or throw away, you may as well know that we have a saying that we found necessary to have embroidered across our chests, "Dare to Dump It!" It was a constant battle to convince each other that what we were saving was ridiculous! In a strong moment of mutual surrender we vowed that if we hadn't cooked with it, danced in it, sat on it, squeezed into it, mailed, read, or watered it in the last twelve months, we never would. The first batch of junk you pitch is the hardest; pretty soon it gets to be fun.

The Put Away box (the "anti-sidetracking device" we mentioned earlier) is for things you will put away in other places, possibly in another room or in a specific drawer as soon as there is room. You'll empty this box as you go along and establish appropriate space for each item.

Storage boxes will accumulate and be put in an area of

the house where they won't be in the way, until you're ready to set up your storage area.

While you clean with the four boxes in tow, make a note about where you could use duplicate cleaning supplies, such as cleanser in each bathroom and the kitchen, broom and dustpan for both kitchen and basement, salt and pepper for the cooking area, as well as for the table.

Establish a mending basket, with glue, needles, assorted thread, tape, etc., and put it by your telephone. Use a shoe box to keep photos that you have stashed and found until you have time to organize them after the house is in order. (Make a card for your file box that says, "Organize Photo Album," and file it several months from now in the January through December dividers.)

It will take the average person at least six weeks to work her way back to the front door. (It took us THREE MONTHS.) Don't be discouraged at how long a job takes. If you work outside your home, figure that it will take you twice as long, or about twelve weeks. No matter how long it takes, be sure to take your FREE DAY every week! (We don't want you to get lost in a closet and set up camp there, mumbling and babbling forever.)

Once you've finished the main part of your house, you'll be ready to start your kitchen. We suggest you organize each area according to its use; wet, hot, cold or dry, which puts your utensils just where you need them. We taped a table-of-contents card to the inside of each kitchen drawer to help keep things in their new places and to keep the drawers from getting scrambled by frantic utensil-seekers.

Each woman has her own special way of arranging things in her kitchen, but we hang our produce in plastic bags in the refrigerator. The fruits and vegetables will stay crisp, in view, and easy to get at, not forgotten and half frozen in the crisper (actually its a slimer) drawer.

In the personal planner we designed, we have a standardized grocery list covered by an acetate sheet. We mark it with a wipe-off pen. When they were still home, we used the kids as coupon cutters. They would gather the products from the supermarket shelves while we shopped. Then we paid them from the "cents off."

After the kitchen, move on to the upstairs, working clockwise from the steps. Then do the basement in the same way, then the garage, clockwise from the garage door.

Remember that this is a long weeding-out process. You didn't get into this mess overnight, and you mustn't expect to get out of it overnight. The *trend* is what's important—a trend toward improvement.

Now you are ready to tackle STORAGE. Read the list of suggested things to store (p. 159). Include any of your own additions or make deletions. Try to streamline the contents of your closets, cupboards, and drawers whenever possible because it will be easier to keep them orderly if they aren't so full. The purpose of a storage area is to clear the main part of the house from seldom or seasonally used items.

When you've cleaned clockwise back to the front door and finished to that point, you'll probably have filled several produce boxes with things to be stored. Now you will start to categorize items and begin filling boxes with similar items, such as all the children's seasonal clothing in one box, all the Halloween costumes, wigs, and masks in another, until each related box is full. There will be items left over that will be too few to be put alone in a box, so they'll go in a Miscellaneous box with other totally unrelated items. (If you wind up with eight hundred boxes marked MISCELLANEOUS, you're doing something wrong.)

As each box is filled, mark it with a letter to represent its category, such as C for clothing and H for Halloween, plus a number to represent which it is in that category. The first box filled with clothing would be marked C-1. If you filled another box in the same category, it would be marked C-2. When starting a new category, such as H for Halloween, mark the first box filled with Halloween costumes H-1, the second box H-2, and the third box H-3.

Fill out one 3×5 white card to correspond to each box (see illustrations, p. 160). Label it with the same letter-number code as its box and include a detailed list of the box's contents, including clothing sizes, colors, amounts, whatever will help you later. File the cards alphabetically in front of the Storage divider in your card-file box.

Now you need to find an area of your house to put the storage boxes. You might want a few different areas, such as keeping holiday decorations in the back of a closet, camping and sporting goods in the garage, and canning equipment in the cupboards above the refrigerator. If you do this, note on each card where its box is located, to avoid confusion. You can create storage areas under stairs, in the garage, in spare-bedroom closets, in the attic, above the low-hanging clothes rack in your children's closet, anywhere there is an out-of-the-way place that will accommodate a few boxes. The produce boxes stack very well, without shelves. They should be stored according to their frequency of use. Put seldom-used things on the highest shelf and frequently needed things lower. Rotate seasonal and holiday boxes according to the time of year. It will save a lot of attic fights with your husband when you establish a storage area. You will never forget what you went through (clutter withdrawal) to get everything nice. Just remember that a S.H.E. is like an alcoholic when it comes to disorder. It's like taking one drink and being gone. If you ever allow yourself to put that first book on top of the dresser, then all of a sudden it's going to have shoes and books and BANANAS on it again.

Knowing our nature, we are consciously aware of every banana we put down. That false convenience of temporarily setting something down to be picked up later is an open gate back to the pigpen.

Memories

*The founders of Sidetracked Home Executives, Inc.
(ages 3½ and 8)*

The most beautiful place on
earth, our childhood home.

Friends forever.

"That's my cake!"

Our dad passed away in 1995. He and Mom had been married 52 years. Mom passed away in 1999. Our loss defies words.

Danny and Peggy.

Terry and Pam.

Our children (from top to bottom): Mike, Peggy, Chris, Joanna, Jeff, and Allyson.

Our adult children and their children (back row from left to right): Michael holding daughter Brooklyn age one, Peggy holding daughter Sophia age nine months, Chris, Joanna, Jeffrey, Allyson. (Front row left to right): Jacob (Peggy's son) age five, McKenzie age five and Hunter age two (Joanna's children), Laura Rose age seven (Jeffrey's daughter).

*Joanna, Chris, and Jeff.
We never knew what
they were going to
be on Halloween ...
until they walked
out the door.*

*Chris and Joanna.
Another last-minute
Halloween. (They
wanted to be vegetables
and this was the best
we could do.)*

*The House Fairy (you'll meet
her on page 92) can be found
even on camping trips.*

Pam and Peggy today.

Regis Philbin, Pam, and Peggy cleaning out purses on AM Los Angeles. *(Photo by Donald Sanders.)*

6

This Little Piggy Stayed Home

It had been four weeks since our first meeting at Eddie's. By now we could see that we would never again allow ourselves to be "The Way We Were" (lyrics, A. Bergman, M. Bergman; music, M. Hamlisch—permission on the way). From the beginning we felt it would be wrong to enlist the help of our husband and children until we could set a standard for orderliness ourselves. How could we have insisted that they make their beds when we were still IN ours? How could we have expected them to set the dinner table if there weren't any clean dishes? We would have felt hypocritical, lecturing them on the importance of getting to school on time when WE were always late. After all, the very reason they'd miss the bus was because of us: no matching socks, no clean underwear (they sometimes wore bathing suits), nothing to make a sack lunch with, and no paper or pen to write a tardy note.

Instead of having homes that were havens of harmony for our loved ones, ours were castles of chaos. Mornings were the worst. We must have been quite a spectacle for the neighbors. When our front doors flew open and everyone scrambled to be the first out the door (nobody was ever on time, but we would all make an effort to be LATE EARLIER), it was like a scene from *Titanic.* Children dashing down the street, half clothed, frantically chasing the bus, hair uncombed, school papers flying. And there we were, racing after them, a banana in one hand and a Pop Tart in the other. "Quick, eat this. It'll hold you till I bring your lunch to school."

Those days were about to fade into our cluttered pasts. We clearly had a challenge in getting our families to be orderly, but we were setting a good example now, and we were ready to begin working with them. We remembered that it took only twenty-one days for us to change a habit. We also reminded each other that age and sex didn't matter. We were determined to turn our little mess-makers into an efficiently organized task force.

We were grateful that, despite the messy surroundings, we had always devoted lots of time to rearing children. Someone once said, "No success can compensate for failure in the home." We didn't regret the time we had given our children. It had been filled consistently with hours of our undivided attention (often at the expense of equally pressing household responsibilities), and we knew we had not failed in showing them life's joys. Now we wanted them to know the joy of order. Our newly established habits were already beginning to rub off on the children; however, we wanted them to go beyond merely obeying orders.

The only time we had ever been organized was when

we had jobs outside of our homes. We realized it was because there were definite guidelines and, with a supervisor there to monitor progress and give encouragement, we were eager to please. Consequently, jobs were completed on time; there was no procrastination; accounts were balanced and desks neatly cleared, all because we had learned to take orders. But following orders proved not to be enough, for, when we were on our own, we had no self-motivation. We hadn't learned to want things nice just to please ourselves, and we could see our children following the same track. We wanted them to realize that having a neat room was for their good as well as for the good of all concerned. We wanted them to see the benefits of hanging up a coat and being spared the frustration of searching frantically for shoes while an irate father sits impatiently in the car, honking the horn. We had suffered enough through horn-honking episodes over the years to last several generations, and we wanted our children to be spared.

They were beginning to feel the peace that accompanied the order we had established so far:

"Mom, where's the Scotch tape?"

"It's in the top drawer of the desk in between the scissors and the box of rubber bands."

"Honey, where's the screwdriver?"

"It's in the tool drawer, rear left-hand corner, beside the pliers."

Now we wanted them to establish order for THEMSELVES.

Since some of our children were quite small, they couldn't be expected to do things as well as the older ones. We realized that, in order to understand the problems in their small world, it would be necessary to get down on their level. We actually got down on our knees to survey our homes from where they stood. (You know the old adage, "Don't tell me you know where a man's been until you've actually smelled his shoes." Or something like that.)

Immediately we realized that we needed to adapt their rooms to their size. Right away we lowered clothes racks in their closets, got *small* hangers for *little* coats, and put hooks inside the closet doors for play clothes. We had watched them struggle and be defeated by dust ruffles, pillow shams, and bunk beds. We decided to make some sacrifices. If you can't part with some of the frills, be prepared cheerfully to help your children arrange them each morning. We also streamlined their dresser drawers—storing clothes that were seasonal in our storage area. We put a step stool in the bathroom so they could easily reach the sink to wash their hands and brush their teeth.

Once we had made things easier for them, we started instilling them with better habits. In the beginning we had to do a lot of policing and training, but it paid off in the long run. We didn't do things *for* them, but *with* them, and gradually things started to improve. If you think your child is too young to know or care that you're disorganized, remember what one of our four-year-olds said when a reporter asked, "Jeff, is your mother really organized now?"

"Yes, she is!"

"Do you know what it means to be organized?"

"Yes, I do. . . . It means that you get up in the morning and you get dressed and make your bed before BREAKFAST instead of before DINNER . . . and you don't have to drink out of jars anymore!"

Children love order and, more important, they love to be the ones responsible for establishing it.

We took the basic idea of our filing system and adapted it for our children. For our youngest (nonreaders), we cut pictures of jobs from magazines, such as a child making his bed or brushing his teeth, and pasted them onto 3×5 cards. At an office-supplies store we bought brightly colored construction paper and had it cut to 3×5 size. On pages 161-162 you'll find a conservative list of what children can be expected to do at various ages. We were amazed at their capabilities once they got motivated. Cutting out the pictures was a lot of fun and aroused their interest in an uncharted zone: HOUSEWORK. Some of our children were more easily interested than others. (Evidently, enough of our husbands' H.E. genes had overpowered our S.H.E. genes because, out of six children, two were BORN ORGANIZED—one was even BORN EARLY—and the other four checked into the world late, as usual.)

"See, Jeffy ... don't *you* want to cut out pictures with Chris, to help you remember your chores?"

"Sure ... I'll cut out the pictures, Mama, but I don't wanna do the work!"

"Hmmm ... "

Next we made a job chart of Naugahyde (so that fingerprints could be easily wiped away) with a pocket sewn on across the top for each child under six. The pictured cards of chores to do were put in each child's pocket. A second row of pockets below the first was for "jobs finished." Our children, who weren't old enough to have the responsibility of a box, worked from the job chart, completing cards and putting them in the pockets below to show they had done their work. Some jobs, such as making the bed, needed to be done first thing in the morning, whereas setting the dinner table was a late-afternoon job. To differentiate the time, we put a half sun for morning jobs, a full sun for afternoon jobs, and a half moon for evening jobs in the upper left-hand corner of the card. We also timed the children at each job and noted the number of minutes spent, in the upper right-hand corner.

We hung the job chart in the children's room, low enough to be within reach. Once in a while we'd stick surprise cards in their pockets, among the work cards, to take them shopping, read a story, go to the zoo, have tickle time, get a quarter for their bank—anything to be an added incentive for them to check their cards first thing in the morning.

Our children six and up have their own file box (regular size instead of jumbo) with seven dividers for the days of the week. Using the list of jobs that children can do, make an Activity List for each child, similar to the one you used for yourself. Include their personal hygiene, homework and outside activities, such as Little League, Scouts, skating lessons, etc., besides their regular chores. You don't need to list the jobs that you already have cards for in your own file box, only the jobs the child alone is responsible for (or should be).

Mark next to each chore on the list how often (daily, weekly, monthly, etc.) it will be done, and estimate the time it will take to finish. Decide which time of day each job will be done, and write on the list either MORNING, AFTER SCHOOL, or BEFORE BED.

Finally, mark which color card to use for each item on the list. Jobs to be done daily go on yellow cards, those to be done weekly on blue cards, and monthly on white. Personal and outside things go on pink cards.

Another divider for EXTRA CREDIT includes white

cards with special weekly, monthly, and occasional jobs printed on them, or a special privilege or activity.

Each night, as we were checking our own next day's cards, we also would take a minute to set up the next day for the children. Some of our own cards, which we had marked "children," were then put in their box—along with one or two extra-credit cards to be done.

If you follow our advice and keep your card file shrouded in mystery, in four weeks your family will be dying to know what's going on! We had our kids begging to have a set of their own cards! Curiosity generates energy. Have you ever noticed that at a parade people will take such great pains to be able to see not only what goes by right in front of them but also what's way up ahead? If you can build up your family's curiosity, they'll have that much more energy to vacuum and wash the car!

When we were ready to introduce the system to our children, we decided to make it a very special occasion. We made invitations to a family-council meeting and mailed one to each member of the family, including our husbands. Children love to receive unexpected mail. (So do husbands. So do wives.) We wanted to spark everyone's enthusiasm for this most important step on our path to order. We had agendas printed so that the first meeting would run smoothly.

It was a little scary, having that first meeting. We wondered if the older children would think it was corny, and we hoped the younger children could sit still for an entire half hour. As usual, our fears were in vain. Our first family-council meetings were smashing successes! We used our tape recorders to record these precious and important events in history, and now wish we had taken movies.

"Is there any new business? . . . Jeff?"

"I think Mom should get a new baby ... and this time try to get a better one than she got the last time!"

(Allyson obviously was bugging him.) "You're out of order, Jeff!"

We discovered that using a tape recorder is not only good for posterity, but it also keeps everyone polite.

That first family-council meeting is crucial! It has to be fun, and yet you have to let your family know that you need their help. We can remember, when we were little, actually wondering what Mom did all day. We visualized her sitting on the sofa with a box of bonbons, kicking around a head of lettuce, and watching TV. We discovered our kids thought the same thing about us! We can logically assume that your children think the same about you.

Once Mava Dinette's husband, Ralph, warned her that there was much work to be done to the house before a party that was rapidly approaching. Mava, busy with planning the food and games for the big event, left the housework until the day of the party. She secretly hired a janitorial service to come and clean for her. It took five men eight hours to bail her out. Ralph came home that evening and said, "Mavey, you did a real good job today. Now, this is how you should keep the place all the time!" Unaware of all the work that goes into cleaning, Ralph just assumed that Mava had put away the bonbons and the head of lettuce, and picked up the vacuum cleaner for a change.

In that first family meeting you need to choose someone to preside. You can let everyone in your family take turns. The leader also gets special privileges all week: sitting in the front seat of the car (the number-one, all-time cause for fights ... "You sat there last time—it's my turn!"), having a friend stay all night, or picking the dessert that is served after the family-council meeting.

There are several things you will want to accomplish in that first meeting. Keep it positive at all times. Help them to feel as you do: that your family, second to God, is all-important. They sometimes need to be reminded of how fortunate they are to be members of their family. You can quicken that feeling of love within each of them by being very loving YOURSELF and telling them how much you care for and appreciate them. It's no coincidence that you have been brought together during your brief stay on this earth. You have been brought together to learn how to love unconditionally, in all circumstances. What a wonderful opportunity to learn!

During the meeting ask your family what they would like to do as a family unit. Plan an outing or activity for the near future. At this point, when you begin asking for ideas and suggestions, it is most important for you to take notes. (There is nothing more flattering than for someone to value your suggestion enough to write it down.) Hand out white 3×5 cards to everyone and ask them to make a list of places they would like to visit, foods they like, things they want, and improvements they would like to see. Collect the cards after the meeting and look them over carefully, discussing them with your husband.

Family-council meetings are the place for all members of the family to air their grievances and criticisms. We allow our children that freedom as long as it is accompanied by respect.

In order to have time to do those things they want to do as a family, explain that everyone has to cooperate. If there is cooperation, there is naturally more time for fun. Plan to spend at least an hour a week with each of your children *alone,* doing just what they like to do. Parents need to have that one-to-one relationship with their children. Sometimes it can be the parent moving into the child's world, and other times it should be the child experiencing the adult world. It should always be high-quality one-to-one time.

As an incentive for the family to keep things neat, introduce the Silent Butler Box at the family-council meeting. Explain that you will give a five-minute warning that the Silent Butler is going to come around. After the warning the butler goes around the house and puts anything left out by anyone in the family into a special Silent Butler Box. (A produce box, decorated in a special way, is great for this.) The items collected will stay in the box until the next family-council meeting, at which time they may be bought back. If your children do not handle money, they can get their possessions back by doing cards of yours that you have decided children can do. (Incidentally, the children can be the butler, too, and if they find anything of yours left out, you get charged.) The best time to send the butler around is right before bedtime and right before everyone leaves for school in the morning. You will discover that it is going to stop most of the unconscious clutter your family is leaving.

There are some wonderful ideas for motivating your children, using a valuable gift they possess: imagination. Imagination can help to make work fun. Emerson said, "It isn't that the nature of a job changes, but that your ability to do increases." He was talking about attitude. We have had days when the thought of housework was welcomed like a stale Oreo and a warm glass of tomato juice. But get a call that someone is coming and there's "instant motivation."

Realizing this trait in ourselves, we had FOR SALE BY OWNER—NO APPOINTMENT NECESSARY signs made to stick in our front lawns on any morning when we woke up with the "I Don't Want to Do Its." We found we could use our children's imaginations to motivate them until they are mature enough to want responsibility.

DING DONG.

"Mike, get the door."

"Hi, there. I'm the House Fairy, and I'm here to check your rooms!"

"Who's there, Mike?"

"It's Aunt Waynee with swim fins and a snow hat on."

"Waynette, what are you doing here, dressed in my old ballet tutu? What are those onions hanging around your neck for? Where did you get that yellow wig and purple lipstick? What's the clipboard for?"

"I'm here to check the kids' bedrooms. I'm gonna check in dresser drawers, under beds, behind doors, and, if the rooms check out, the kids get a special treat."

The House Fairy was an instant success. The children scattered to their rooms to make sure they would get a surprise. We decided to take turns being the House Fairy. Once a month she comes unannounced and does a complete check. If you don't have a crazy sister who will dress up in absurd clothes to call on your children, you can have an imaginary House Fairy who comes, like the Tooth Fairy, and leaves tiny notes under pillows, in pockets, etc., and leaves tiny treats, such as Tic-Tacs and M&Ms.

We have such wonderful times shocking each other and seeing who can come up with the most outrageous version of the infamous House Fairy. We think that

sometimes, as adults, we get too serious about life. Maybe when we learn how to control our emotions, we somehow get the idea that we have to become serious. Our children enjoy seeing us be silly, and we enjoy it, too. We have discovered that joy is a wonderful way to bring a family closer together.

Laugh with your children. Look for the humor in every situation because it's there if you can only recognize it. Step back from difficulties so that you can look into them more objectively. Remember how funny a situation is once it's in the past and you've realized everything worked out fine in the end. The passing of time takes the sting out of all disasters. In the middle of a crisis, if you can get that distance that time affords, whether by counting to ten or leaving the room. There were times, when our children were young, when we considered it a good day if at the end of it everyone was accounted for. Do whatever it takes to step back and see the humor or the blessing. If it's not immediately clear, believe that it will be someday, whether you know it or not.

Ranting and raving, whining and nagging, are the things that break down communication. When you write out the chores that need to be done, you eliminate constant nagging. Nobody likes to be told over and over to do a job (especially when one adult is telling another). It's much simpler and more effective to have everything written on cards. The written word has so much more authority than the voice of a wife or mother. Whatever you want, put it in writing.

Finally, ENJOY your family! Now is the only time you'll all be living together, and it's such an important, yet fleeting, time. Let everything you do with your family become a beautiful memory.

7

'Twas the Night Before Christmas

DATE: December 22, 1977
SCENE: Eddie's Villa del Weenie

We stopped by the Villa for a bite to eat after a leisurely shopping trip. With three days until Christmas, Eddie's was bustling with the excitement of the holiday season. Twelve-inch taco shells sprayed with glitter hung from the ceiling. The giant bull, converted temporarily into a reindeer, circled the restaurant, dragging a sleigh filled with Christmas treats. It was the one time of the year that Eddie came out of the kitchen, dressed as—you guessed it—Babe Ruth.

The children flocked around him, awaiting the chance to recite their Christmas lists and ride the bull, while we relaxed over coffee.

"I had a ball shopping, didn't you?"

"Yeah."

"Did you see that woman pawing through the table of half-price mittens?"

"Yeah, she was wild. I know just how she felt, though."

"Me, too. I looked into her eyes, and I could see that same panic we had last Christmas. I can remember praying, 'O Lord, bless my desperate search for those twenty-five gifts I need to find in two hours. Let there be cash somewhere I haven't looked, and let my bank card work one more time without an authorization call. Let there be just one more Polly Puberty Doll somewhere, and let there be batteries included. Guide me to just the right store, and lead me to the correct sizes and colors. Let each selection be exactly what my loved ones had hoped and dreamed for. Keep me calm as I grope through crowds, scrounge through sale items, and dash up and down escalators. O Lord, forgive me for leaving this to the last minute again. If you'll get me through this one more time, I promise I'll get organized.' "

"I've said that exact prayer. Think of her having a brat on top of it."

"She had a brat?"

"Yeah. Didn't you see that kid hanging by his knees off the coatrack?"

"No."

"Well, he was. She had him on a leash until he forced her to take it off."

"How old was he?"

"About three."

"Can you imagine letting your three-year-old hang by his knees off a coatrack?"

"No, but that's not all he did."

"Oh, spare me."

"He took all his clothes off and sent them up the escalator, one piece at a time."

"You're kidding."

"I'm not kidding. I enjoyed watching the stuff go up almost as much as he did."

"You watched him?"

"Yeah, it was great—made me feel lucky I had at least worked on the kids' behavior in public. You know our kids are so well trained all we have to do is give them the fish eye and they know they'd better shape up."

"Sissy, I think the fish eye is in order."

"Why?"

"Look at Jeff—he's hanging candy canes on the bull's horns."

"Jeffrey, get those canes off the bull."

"Listen, I've gotta get home."

"Me, too. I'll see you tomorrow."

On our way to our homes, we each thought about what we had missed in Christmases past because of our lack of organization. We recognized that, if the Home Executives of the world (those born organized) were going crazy at Christmastime, it was no wonder *we* had always spent the holidays in shock.

We loved Christmas. It had always been the most joyous time of the year for us. We sensed that subtle but so real essence that fills everyone with a special love for humanity. We had visions of welcoming friends and loved ones into our homes to share the blessedness of the season. Christmas was supposed to be our favorite time of year. We should have been decking the halls with boughs of holly and co-directing extravagant scenes from the Nativity. We always would jump into festivities head-first. After all, we were creating memories our children would cherish all their lives:

"Where are the camel costumes we started making last year?"

"I don't know. Let's look up in the attic."

"OK ... Hey, the light's out up here."

"Oh, shoot, we're out of bulbs. Just a sec and I'll get the flashlight. ... OK, who put a Playtex nurser nipple on the flashlight, and where are the batteries? What do you mean, they're in Gertie Gezundheit? Sissy, are you still up there?"

"Yeah, but I've stepped in something!"

"Sissy, I think it's the ceiling. I can see your foot!"

Every year we pictured ourselves, cheerful and relaxed, logs on the fire, our cozy homes filled with the warm glow of spicy candles and the aroma of freshly baked Christmas treats. We wanted our homes to be bustling with excitement, an open invitation for all passersby to drop in and share the Christmas spirit.

We wanted to be FREE to reflect on the blessings the holiday symbolizes. Ha! We were raving maniacs! We began our holiday preparations on December 20 and always expected miracles. We wanted everything to be perfect—the tree, the dinner, the house, the children—and nothing ever was. We'd get a scrawny tree because all the good ones had been picked over; dinner was always late, and one night before Christmas, this was the way it was:

'Twas the night before Christmas, not long ago.
We were sidetracked then, as you now know.
The stockings weren't hung by the chimney like most.
The presents weren't wrapped; no chestnuts to roast.
The children were sleeping in summer pajamas,
'Cause the box full of flannels was over at Grama's.
With Dad in his T-shirt, and I in one too,
I just couldn't sleep. I had too much to do.
For out on the lawn was a horrible clutter,

'Cause two days before I had cleaned out the gutter
To see if the Christmas-tree lights were still there.
Now the lawn was a mess, but the gutter was bare.
The moon on the breast of junk on the lawn
Caused me to know I'd be up until dawn.
Away to the kitchen I flew like a flash!
Tore open the oven, where the dishes were stashed.
I pulled out the dishes, turned the oven on bake;
I had nut breads and cookies and puddings to make.
I opened the freezer and filled up with fear,
For what to my wondering eyes should appear?
But the turkey, still frozen—what else could we eat?
Could I pass off these fish sticks as a holiday treat?
More rapid than eagles I shut the door.
I sobbed and whimpered and fell to the floor.
With the wink of an eye and the twist of my head,
I figured I'd bag it and flop into bed.
But then in a twinkling I heard a small knock.
It was Sissy. (She lived down the street just a block.)
She was dressed all in fur from her head to her boots,
And she carried a basket of half-eaten fruits.
"Why are you dressed like the jolly old elf?"
And I laughed when I saw her, in spite of myself.
She spoke not a word but went straight for my throat,
And then what she said, I don't think I should quote!
"I came over to tell you the kids wrecked my fruit,
"And I haven't finished your gift, it's a suit.
"Oh, Sissy," she wailed, "I'm really behind.
"I've got cards to address and stockings to find."
"Your holiday centerpiece isn't so jerky;
"It won't matter anyway; we don't have a turkey!
"It's frozen and I'm so ashamed and upset.
"Christmas is not what I want to regret.

"I want to have order and peace in this place,
"Have laughter and singing, a smile on my face."
Laying a finger aside of our nose,
We vowed we would change from our heads to our
*   toes.*
We sprang to our senses and both gave a whistle.
Our hairdos both looked like the down of a thistle.
But we knew very soon in some wonderful way
The answer would come on one glorious day!
You can hear us exclaim, though we're out of your sight,
"Merry Christmas to all, and to all a good night!"

It turned out that that was the last Christmas we spent eating at Eddie's and *wishing* we had gone to church after eating turkey and fresh pumpkin pie. What a pleasure to kiss Christmas chaos GOOD-BYE!

Even the most organized Home Executive can find entertaining a challenge. The poor little Sidetracked Home Executive (unreformed) finds that her lack of order takes all the joy out of entertaining. Instead of enjoying the spiritual nature of a sacred holiday, she finds her finances strained, her nerves on edge, and her desire to do good vanishing in a sea of all the extra activity.

If you make a decision to get organized, and that decision happens to come during the holidays, believe it or not, it is a blessing. NOW you really have something to celebrate. NOW you truly have a gift to give your family. If you've decided that this is the time to change your life and get organized, you need our

H.E.L.P.
(Holiday Emergency List of Priorities)

1. *Forgive yourself!* See that your intentions have al-

ways been good. Realize that your motives have been pure, and don't panic.

2. Realize that in deciding to change, the tangible effects of that decision won't show up immediately. Remember that philosopher William James, who said to change your attitude, and your circumstances also will change.

3. *Celebrate* the change in your attitude. Rejoice in knowing that things are going to be different, and it will be for the good of all concerned.

4. Call an emergency family-council meeting and explain how you feel and how you have felt every Christmas. You owe it to yourself and your family to share your feelings. If in those chaotic Christmases past we had let go of our pride and confided our feelings, we would have had some wonderful times. We wanted Christmas to be as it was when we were little. Mom, being so organized, was free to do the *extra* things that make Christmas such a wonderful time of year. Our home was decorated like a department-store window, with the center being the most gorgeous tree we had ever seen. The excitement, the love, the Christmas Spirit, it was all there, nothing was missing, and we wanted our families to remember Christmas in the same way. If we could have shared that, we would have been amazed at the results. Whenever we have taught our class around the holidays, we give our students this H.E.L.P. and we have miracle testimonies.

5. Expect a miracle. Ask for your family's help and joyfully accept it. In one family the husband took over the entire Christmas-card list. Teenagers volunteered to plan and fix the dinner, and the younger children decorated the tree with their precious school artwork. Our students said it was the worst-looking tree they had ever had, but

visitors couldn't help but feel the warmth and love in the home, and the children were bursting with pride.

See how many "things" you can eliminate this Christmas and yet still get that "feeling" you want. The gifts of life are really feelings, not things. Make this a FEELING CHRISTMAS instead of a HAVING CHRISTMAS.

During the holiday season it's important to eliminate certain household chores so that you can be free to concentrate on special holiday activities. Eliminate such jobs as cleaning the baseboards, putting down new shelf paper, cleaning drapes, etc. There is a time to get to those jobs, and the holidays are not the time. You will need to have a clean refrigerator, oven, kitchen, bathroom, and living room.

Go over the suggested Christmas Activity List (see Appendix, p. 152). Personalize it to fit your family. Fill in the date each activity will need to be started. Estimate how much time will be required (if the activity can be done in ten minutes or less, or if it can be divided into ten-minute segments to be worked on as time allows, mark the MINI column). Delegate as much as possible to your husband, children, and get the entire family involved. Finally, decide when each activity will need to be completed.

Buy heavy, bright green paper at a stationery store and have it cut to 3×5 size, to fit in your file box. Transfer all the things you want to do for the holidays onto the 3×5 cards, one activity per card, just as we did with the Basic Activity List for your house. Write on the cards the information you've written on the list. File the cards in front of your Christmas divider or in front of the appropriate month that specific projects will need to be started by. Fill out the gift list (see Appendix, pp. 153-154). This will help you keep trac of everyone on it.

Gift-giving for Christmas always threw us into the biggest dither, and left us knowing that we'd be shopping madly on December 24. To eliminate that, figure out how much time is left until December. (Again, we recommend starting in January.) Divide the time left, whether it be weeks, months, or days, *into* the number of people on your Christmas-gift list. The result will be the number of gifts you must buy or make in the remaining time until Christmas.

Buying or making gifts throughout the year saves you mental and financial strain in December. It also gives you the time and peace of mind to think of just the right gift for each person—often on sale—instead of buying everybody on your list a board of assorted cheese wedges gaily surrounded by Easter grass, or the Nut Whacker (by We R Nuts) as seen on TV.

On the first Christmas after we got organized, it was wonderful to see our children exchanging gifts. For the first time, their attention was on GIVING instead of receiving, and we had time to supervise. Peggy Ann bought three inexpensive children's books and blank cassette tapes to go with each book. She read the books into the tape recorder and, when it was time to turn the page, she rang a crystal bell and said, "OK, Chris, it's time to turn the page." The stories were interspersed with her own personal comments and were the delight of all our preschoolers.

To avoid all-night wrapping sessions on Christmas Eve, we suggest that you keep a produce box in a convenient closet for holding wrapping paper, clothing folders (which we ask for every time we buy clothes in specialty stores), bows, tags, tape, scissors, etc. Wrap the presents immediately after you buy or make them, to resist the temptation of giving them for birthdays, anniversaries, or graduations. Once a gift is wrapped and tagged, check it off on your gift list in the column provided. On the back of the gift tag, put a number instead of a name. The number will correspond to a master list on a 3×5 card, which you'll put in front of the Christmas divider in your file box. The master list will assign a number to each package and a description of the contents of each gift (or you might forget what you bought.) (See Appendix, p. 159.)

Wrapping the presents right away and giving them numbers instead of names helps keep peeking children at bay. But if kids are *really* sneaky, they might be bright enough to look for the master list in your card file. If so, mislabel the card JUNK TO TAKE TO THE DUMP.

We also recommend making out separate 3×5 gift cards for each member of your family and noting requests they make during the year. It's a good idea to buy gifts for your immediate family last, since usually you will be buying more for them, and they are the easiest to shop for. That's especially true for children, who are constantly telling you exactly what they want—straight from all the Christmas-toy commercials.

We take each of our children on a Dream Day before Christmas. Each child gets a separate day when we go shopping, without buying anything. They get a chance to see all the toys firsthand, touch, if possible, and make their "Santa List."

A final word: Keep your sales receipts in front of your Christmas divider in case returns are necessary.

Take time out to reflect and give thanks for the blessings you share with your family. You are a unique expression of life itself. Celebrate that part within you that is ever pressing to express THROUGH you as Love, Laughter, Peace, and (yes) Order, and have a Merry Christmas.

8

This Little Piggy Gets a Mouse

The computer can be a wonderful tool to help you get organized and stay on track. When we got our acts together back in 1977, computers were only in banks. Back then Bill Gates was fighting acne, and just beginning to tinker with ideas that would change the world. Words like windows, mouse, cookies, and web were household words before any household had a personal computer.

We both ventured into the computer world with Commodore 64s, and comparing their memory to the memory of the computers we have today is like comparing the memory of Forrest Gump with Einstein's. It is fantastic what can be done today because of this wonderful technology. We originally used our computers to write our books, but as we became more familiar with the capabilities of a computer we discovered a great new tool for staying on track. We said earlier that the only thing a

Sidetracked Home Executive lacks is direction. The 3×5 cards give direction. They tell what has to be done. It's almost like having your mom right there saying, "Betty, set the table." One of a sidetracker's strengths is her ability to follow directions. (It's probably because wanting to please fits in there somewhere.) It's one thing to have a 3×5 card tell you what to do and quite another to have a computer order you around. There is something so business-like about a computer readout. It's more like having your father tell you what to do!

If you decide you want to use your computer in place of 3×5 cards, we are sure you will love the results. Instead of putting the activities that are on the activity list on 3×5 cards, you will put them into a software program. Every day we get calls from S.H.E.s wondering if we sell a software program. We even had a computer wizard ask to work on one for us, but he was too expensive. He did cause us to check out the market and see what was out there. We found that there are many programs and it has been a matter of finding the best one to suit our system and the needs of easily sidetracked people. The one we like the best seems perfect for our system. It's called Lotus Notes R5 by Lotus and the cost is moderate, about $30.

Lotus comes with a fun beginner's guidebook. A friendly man's loafer named Sherman takes the beginner on a tour of the program by leaving a trail of footprints from one page to the next. The nice shoe explains each section in very easy-to-understand terms. If the beginner has questions along the way the cute little shoe is happy to answer each of them. Sherman actually has a very good sense of humor! In the beginning of the guidebook he suggests that you close the door to your office so that others won't think you're crazy talking to a shoe in a book.

Since we recommend Lotus Notes R5, we will use it as the example for putting our system to work on your computer. Please note that we are not sponsors of this software program and we are not trying to sell it specifically. There are many programs on the market. ACT 2000 works very well with our system but the cost is about $180. If you want to shop around, ask the sales person at your favorite computer store for the most popular database program. Be sure the program has a calendar, a task or to-do list and appointment making capabilities. We suggest that you check out all the options especially because of the rapid rate of new information in the technology world.

It doesn't surprise us that we have been unable to find a software program that was created specifically for running an efficient home. Every software product we've looked at is geared for running an efficient business, including Lotus Notes R5. Since we consider running a home a business (the most important business on earth), we just pretend those software programs think that too.

When we created our 3×5 system we borrowed the concept from *The Columbian,* our hometown newspaper. Peggy worked at the paper in display ads. When she got the job, her boss gave her a card file full of 3×5 cards with the names and telephone numbers of customers who advertised regularly. He called it a rotating tickler file that was used by many businesses at that time. The card file had dividers labeled Monday through Friday. She was to call the customers regularly to see if they wanted to place an ad. If a company advertised weekly the card reminded her to call weekly. If a customer advertised every other day that card would show up every other day. It was an epiphany to realize that tasks in a home were just like those customers needing to place an ad. Housework is repetitive. It is if you do it!

In today's world, it is increasingly difficult to keep track of all the things you need to do. At home alone, there are projects to complete, information to find, phone calls to make, letters to write, meetings to attend, and if you have a husband and kids you are most likely working for them too. If you also work outside your home, managing all the things you have to do can be overwhelming. When we tweaked Lotus Notes R5 to fit our homemaking requirements and the responsibilities of running our company, we were thrilled with the results. On Tuesday we might have a meeting with the toilet as well as one with our agent. Some of the jobs in a home require meetings daily, some weekly, some every other month, just like in a business. When we run out of time, we reschedule meetings, send someone else, or cancel entirely. Once you see that a home is no different than a business, then you are ready to put our system to work on your computer.

Before you run out and buy an organizer program, we want to warn you that we are assuming that you are comfortable using a computer and would like to go to your keyboard instead of a card file box. If you are afraid of your computer, then perhaps you should stick with the card file box.

We were also a little leery about writing this chapter and giving our Sidetracked Sisterhood permission to use a personal computer as a tool for getting organized. There are two reasons we worried. One was the easy access to games like Tetris, Mindsweep, solitaire and the millions of playtime programs available. For example, you could have every intention of turning on your computer in the morning to print out your calendar of activities for the day when something in your right brain says, *"Let's play just one game of Hearts."* Before you know what happened you could be in a serious tournament with yourself and getting your life organized is deleted from your mind. We suggest that if you're going to use your computer, until you reach your goal of having your life organized, have someone hide the games somewhere in the bowels of your hard drive. Then when you feel you can handle the temptation of the games, you can bring them back. We both had to have the games hidden and although the procedure isn't painless it has saved us hours when we were supposed to be writing.

The Internet is the other pitfall, although if used properly it can truly guide you in your endeavor to get organized. We have a wonderful Web site with motivation; inspiration, and actual chat rooms you can go to and talk with other Sidetracked Home Executives. It's a great place to find a cyber partner or be motivated to join hourly challenges to get tasks accomplished and report back. You can also find out what we are up to on our Web site www.shesintouch.com. We feel it's an extension of our own homes and our front door is always open. Once you come into our cyber-home we have created many threads whereby you can find other sites to help you with organization.

We have had our Web site for six years and we've learned a lot from the people who frequent it. They have given us input about computer-related questions and we've come up with some important points to consider when using your computer and our system together.

Using a Software Organizing Program with the S.H.E. System

1. If you have decided you have the willpower to use your computer to help you and your family become organized and you promise to lose the games and limit your time chitchatting on the Internet, then choose a software program that has these features: a calendar, to-do list, appointments, and address book. The Lotus Notes R5 program has a calendar and task tracker. The calendar lets you schedule and track your activities and reminds you where you need to be and when you need to be there. The task tracker lets you create and track your "To-Do" list. You can display items from your "To-Do" list on your calendar as well. The calendar and task tracker are both in the Lotus Notes R5 database.

2. Install the software of your choice. We weren't computer savvy enough to install the program, but once it was up and running we fell in love with Lotus Notes R5.

3. Read through all the jobs on the activity list in the appendix that starts on page 136 of this book. Customize the list to meet your requirements. You can change frequencies, add or omit jobs, and write more detailed descriptions of jobs, etc.

4. Create a weekly plan. (See page 155 to remember the importance of a weekly plan.)

5. With this book and your weekly plan in front of you, follow the directions given with your software program for entering all the data. An important note: Lotus Notes R5 allows you to put specific times when you enter information in the appointment section.

Any tasks you want to have a specific time denoted (like shower, dress, hair, and makeup 7:00–7:30) enter it in the appointment section. Tasks that don't need a specific time can be entered in the to-do list section. Once you have entered every task and given a frequency, the program is ready to work for you. All you do is go to the calendar section and on any given day all the jobs that you programmed in for that day will appear. The software program lets you enter frequencies, so that the tasks keep reappearing for as long as you want them to. Feeding the activities into the computer will save you hours of time you would spend making out 3×5 cards. Once all the data is programmed into your computer, you will go to it instead of a card file.

6. Have fun customizing the look of your pages. Most computer software has color and design choices as well as choices of lettering known as fonts. (If you thought a font was a receptacle for holy water, better get a pack of 3×5s and a pen, snuggle up to the potbelly stove, light the lamp, and get organized the old-fashioned way.) You'll enjoy making your organizing pages unique, but watch your time. You could end up spending weeks working on just the right look, and your home could sink deeper into chaos and confusion.

7. If you use a day planner like the one we have developed, you can set your computer to print out pages that will fit in your planner. Lotus Notes R5 gives you the choice to have pages that fit our organizer or other sizes currently on the market.

Remember that a computer is a tool. It's not going to do the work for you. We Sidetrackers love to play and we can get very excited about a project. The thought of getting the house streamlined; meals on time; closets, cupboards, and drawers cleaned out; and turning a chaotic life into a peaceful one is tempting. We Sidetracked Home Executives are the most thoughtful people in the world, but sometimes all we do is think about it. Whether you get a software program, use a personal planner, or use a 3 × 5 card file, once you have it all planned out *then* you have to do the work. It will be the most rewarding project you will ever undertake and we praise you in advance for being successful.

What's It All About?

*I*t was three years ago to the day that we sat crying into the guacamole dip and taco chips, and confessed our shortcomings as homemakers. We smiled at each other now on this third anniversary marking our triumph. We had done it! We had mastered that which had been our cross to bear. Somehow, by being absolutely at the end of our ropes (if we'd been able to find them) and having the desire to change, we had been willing to try anything. We had prayed for an answer for all the years that we had lived apart from each other. But it wasn't until we were reunited that our answer came. Why?

We had wondered at times during the past year why the solution to our problem, which had eluded us for so many years, unfolded so easily and perfectly in the course of five weeks. Why? Why had we suffered so when the answer was contained within us? Why hadn't we thought of it earlier and spared ourselves the guilt,

---

115

embarrassment, and anxiety that accompanies disorder? Now we *knew* why, as we reflected over the past three years and where they had led us. We had taken a problem that seemed hopeless, and challenged it—and we had won!

Only through EXPERIENCING the problem could we know and understand what it's like to be a disorganized person. In the same way that a drug addict finds hope from a person who is no longer on drugs, but resents the well-meaning lectures of someone who's never even taken an aspirin, so it was with the millions of disorganized women we would be able to reach in total understanding and love.

It had been three years since we had begun coming weekly to Eddie's, children in tow, with blank paper and pens, wondering what to do next. When we left the restaurant each time, we would be so full of excitement and enthusiasm that we actually felt feverish. There was absolutely no doubt in either of our minds that the system would work, and if it would work for two such "terminal slobs" as us, it would work for ANYONE. We had prayed to be open channels for the answers we needed, and as we looked back over the work of the past three years, we were amazed at what had been accomplished. It went *far beyond anything we alone could take credit for.* We had taught nearly 155,000 people the system. We employed sixteen teachers, all with the same impressive credentials we had: "slob successfully reformed." Our book was completed. We had received national exposure in magazines and on television, to the amazement and disbelief of public-relations people.

Gradually, in that three years, it was made very clear to us that we alone were not responsible for what was happening. We are thankful to our Creator for helping us change the climates in our homes and giving us the privilege of sharing what we learned.

The lessons sometimes have been rocky ones. Each of us feels the need to share what has happened in her home because we know thousands of people are facing many of the same things we had to face.

FROM PAM

Peggy and I were brought up in a home that shielded us from unhappy people and unhappy situations. We never heard our parents raise their voices to each other. They had disagreements, but they settled grievances as two mature, loving people should. After fifty-two years of marriage they enjoyed each other even more.

Until the age of twenty I had never been away from home. I was unprepared to meet a sometimes harsh world. I guess I thought almost everyone had been brought up as Peggy and I had been. I remember having my feelings hurt every time I turned around. I was prepared to be a good parent because of the examples I had in my parents. But I wasn't ready for marriage because I saw it as an extension of the protection I had while I was growing up. Everybody my age was rushing to get married. Mom was married when she was nineteen, so I was already one year over the hill. In 1963 I walked down the aisle. My bridegroom was gorgeous! He had the cutest-shaped head, pretty teeth, blue-green eyes with eyelashes a foot long, Tom Hanks hair, and a perfect body. Beauty was not one of my own assets. We had absolutely nothing in common. He loved to lift weights, jog, and sunbathe for hours. I got a D in P.E. (my only one ever) and hate to sweat; in the sun my body goes through three phases: burn, peel, freckle. To supplement his income I wanted to write children's books, write songs, paint, design clothes, do anything creative. He wanted me to be a meat wrapper. (He'd heard that the Meat Wrapper's Union provided good benefits.)

I got married out of need. I needed someone to take care of me, someone I could lean on. I had very few opinions of my own. I didn't want the responsibility of making decisions, for fear someone would criticize me. Instead of getting to the root of my problem by myself, I unconsciously used another person so that I would not have to grow up. As long as I was looking for security in someone else, I was tabling the inner work I would eventually have to do.

If you look to someone else for your happiness, your success, your security, or whatever you think you need, you will wake up one day and find you have been on a merry-go-round. The day you realize that you are responsible for creating your own pleasure or pain, success or failure, strength or weakness, is the day you are truly free, for you are no longer at the mercy of what other people do. You discover that the search for happiness, success, and peace of mind is an inner search.

I believe that if you understand yourself—when you see that it's your responsibility to be happy and that no one else is going to do it for you—then, and only then, are you in a position to have a meaningful relationship with another person who has the same level of self-awareness. It's such a joy to share your love for life with people who love life in a similar way. It comes, then, to a choice to be with someone and a willingness to accept him as he is.

I always thought that a marriage would be successful if it was based on love. But there has to be more than love, believe it or not. If you look back on your life, and if you are a loving person, you will see that you have loved lots of people. If you love easily, you have easily recognized the good in hundreds of people. Since you can't be married to everyone you love, the basis for marriage has to go beyond love. It's a commitment to be involved with another person, to enter into that agreement with no conditions placed on each other. The "I'll love you if" kind of agreement is for children. The fewer "I'll love you ifs" you have, the happier you'll be, sharing your life and love with someone else.

You are responsible for your choices. Choices are what have brought you to this point in your life. If you choose to set up camp on a live volcano, be prepared to get burned. If you get burned and decide to move, be sure you understand why you chose to camp on the volcano in the first place, and resolve it before you move on—or you're liable to set up camp on another volcano.

If you made a wrong choice, something within you will keep nudging you. Life has a way of telling you when you are on the right track ... it's called joy. If your motive for getting married was wrong, chances are your marriage isn't working. Don't get hung up on the spiritual meaning of the marriage ceremony if your reasons for getting married weren't spiritual.

When I came face to face with what I was doing with my life, I realized I was compromising. I was being less than I could be, and I knew my capacity for happiness and success was far greater than I could express in the situation I had gotten myself into. I was married for fourteen years. I kept thinking things would get better. I can remember telling myself to keep a calendar of good days versus bad days. But I was so terribly disorganized that I was lucky to know what month it was, let alone keep track of whether it had been a good or bad day.

Shakespeare said, "There is nothing either good or bad, but thinking makes it so." Through those years of incompatibility, I always had an overabundance of optimism. I was frequently accused of living in a dream world. I was offended at the accusation, but one day I realized that it was a compliment. We all live in dream worlds. Emerson said, "Things are not as they are, but as we are." How we perceive the world is the world we live in. Some people go from crisis to crisis, whereas others go from one wonderful experience to another. If you are a happy, optimistic person, enjoy your dream world. If your optimism backs you into a corner, it will certainly get you out, too, and you will have grown in the experience.

Marriage should be based on *mutual sharing*, not mutual dependency.

When you realize that you are responsible for your own happiness, then you will also see that you are not responsible for someone else's happiness. If someone continually places demands on you in an effort to be happy, you have the right to know that you can decline. If you have discovered that you are depending on your mate for your happiness or on his strength because of your weakness, you need to see that sooner or later you must face your faults and fears alone.

It sounds terribly scary, but if you will step out in faith, you will find that you really aren't alone. There is a power and wisdom right within you to meet every challenge. Whatever your fears are, the only really frightening thing is fear itself.

Someone has said, "When you realize no one has the

power to hurt you, you will be like a bird perched on a branch. If the branch breaks, why fear? The bird can fly." In my family no one ever said the word "divorce," let alone got one! I was standing on the "what will people think" branch, and when it broke, I found I could fly:

"Sissy, I am going to get a d . . ."

"What?"

"I'm going to get a di . . ."

"A what?"

"A divorce. What will they say when they see it in the newspaper?"

"Who's they?"

"You know: everybody who knows me."

"Anybody in particular?"

"Yeah. Our neighbor, John Marshall; Mrs. Prescott, my fifth-grade teacher; and the Reverend Don."

"Don't you care what the rest of them think?"

"No."

"Well, then, call each one and tell them how you feel. Tell them that when they read about it in the paper, you'll be so embarrassed. Tell them you feel that you've failed and that they'll probably hate you for the rest of your life, but you hope someday they will find it in their hearts to forgive you, and maybe one day they will be able to pass you on the street without spitting on you. Just tell them (all three of them) that you are sorry you're doing this, and you hope they can find the strength and courage to go on with their lives now that they know how miserably *you've* failed. Oh, and tell them that you're organized now, and maybe you just might impress one of them."

After my wise little sister put it in the proper perspective, I had learned another valuable lesson. I didn't have to call anybody, and I didn't care what *they* thought.

I remember through the years thinking how embarrassing it would be if I did get a divorce. I couldn't bear to have it appear in the divorce announcements.

Life has a way of showing us how silly our fears really are. For one thing, when the announcement came out, Peggy and I were in Chicago. In fact, I never did see it. Several months later Peggy and I were interviewed by the *Oregonian* newspaper. The story was on the first page of the women's section and the headline, which was at least an inch high, read: NOTORIOUS SLOBS SWEEP HOMES CLEAN—INCLUDING ONE HUSBAND.

I was always criticized for maintaining the messiest house in the world. The criticism was justified. After all, I was a full-time homemaker and he never knew when he'd get a meal or what he'd have to wear.

In our fourteen years of marriage, most of our fights were over the mess. I must say, I know what it's like to feel guilty for being such a slob. I wanted to change during all those years of our marriage so that the criticism would stop. I had allowed this criticism of my housekeeping to affect how I felt about myself. There were many times during our marriage that I felt absolutely worthless. I felt like a failure.

When your self-esteem begins to lower, you cannot see any good in yourself. I began to think I was a failure as a mother, when I wasn't. I began feeling guilty about doing volunteer work for the school and church. I even began feeling uneasy when I took that vitally important time to commune with God.

Disorder affects every area of your life. It can ruin a good marriage and douse any hope for a troubled marriage. Your finances, your social life, EVERYTHING is affected by disorder.

People like us (Sidetracked Home Executives) with our flexible natures, are also easily persuaded. We need to learn to stand strong when our character is being judged. We must *never* allow anyone to *stifle* our love for our life. We have a right to be, whether we're messy or not. We have a right to spend time smelling the roses and talking to puppies. We can play with kittens and babies, watch spiders build webs, and sing our praises to a sunset. We can dance when the music plays and dare to dream! The wonderful thing about being organized FIRST is that you HAVE MORE TIME TO DO THE THINGS YOU LOVE.

I must say that I did NOT get organized to prove a point. When I began to improve, the criticism didn't stop. Gradually I realized that critical people are critical people, and I stopped taking it personally. I began to be indifferent to the criticism in an attempt to keep my own spirits high. Out of a necessity to stay positive, I blanked out all negative influence. The complaints became like a radio on the wrong station; I was no longer an audience. Gradually my indifference changed from a willful, conscious effort to ignore the criticism to an actual indifference to it. I really didn't care anymore. I realized that I didn't want to share my life experiences with a critical person.

Things couldn't have been worse that last year of my marriage. Everything had crumbled within our relationship, yet I had never been happier and more fulfilled. As my self-image improved and I was no longer financially dependent on him, the bubble burst. Divorce can be a very positive thing, especially if you are a positive person. My mom said to me after the whole thing was over,

"You must be so much happier now." I could honestly say to her that I didn't get a divorce so that I'd be happier. In fact, I knew I would be just exactly the way I was in that last year of marriage. My confidence was so improved as I realized I had control over a problem that had haunted me my whole life: lack of organization.

Please don't get your act together to prove to someone else that you can do it. Do it for yourself. Know that when you change something within yourself for the good, only good can come from that change. A change for good within you is automatically for the good of everyone else with whom you come in contact. You have a perfect right to have a harmonious life. Your home can be a place where flowers bloom, children laugh, and music fills the air.

I have many questions about life, but I know one thing: We were created for joy. A great spiritual teacher, Paramahansa Yogananda, said in one of his poems, "From Joy I came, for Joy I live, and in sacred Joy I melt." Be happy where you are, within yourself, and you will be a light to others in a world that needs more joy.

Oral Roberts said, "Your life is a gift from God. What you do with that life is your gift back to God." Give the best that is in you, and you will be happy. Have a love affair with life!

FROM PEGGY

Danny and I were married in May of 1967. Fourteen days after our wedding he was sent with the 173rd Airborne Division to Vietnam, where he spent the next thirteen months. I felt as if we'd had such a short time together, as if we'd gone on a big, scandalous date, and then he brought me back to my parents' house and left.

During that year he lived in conditions that would have been unbearable to me. I vowed that when he came back I would be a wonderful wife and do everything in my power to have our home perfect for him.

It was a promise I didn't keep. Although I loved to cook, meals were never on time. I loved feminine things, dresses, makeup, delicate jewelry and perfume, but at some point I'd stopped wearing them. I loved to go out with Danny to the movies or to dinner, but I was never on time, much to his irritation. I wanted to make life at home easy and comfortable, but in all the clutter and disorder, our home was tense, and it was difficult for him to relax. I tried to make up for all my shortcomings by being affectionate and lighthearted.

After putting up with five years of running out of toilet paper and finding empty toothpaste tubes, damp underwear, no handkerchiefs, wrinkled shirts, cat hair on his police uniform, lukewarm TV dinners, and overdrafts—not to mention a home that he was embarrassed to have friends visit unexpectedly, and a wife who always wore a scarf on her head, no makeup, and the same old ratty pants and striped shirt—our marriage was in real trouble. He told me finally, "I'm not happy."

We visited a marriage counselor and were told to make a list of the things we liked and disliked about each other. The list was not to be shared with each other but was to be *totally confidential.*

I ransacked his desk drawer and found his list (I'm so ashamed), and it was very puzzling to me. The list of things that he liked about me was a long one. It had all the virtues you'd expect of a saint: honest, faithful, kind, affectionate, loves children, joyful, good sense of humor (doesn't brag about virtues—oops, I added that myself), etc. I thought, "Wow, if I'm all those things to him, how come he's not happy with me?"

Then I turned the list over to the "don't likes" and found at the top of the list "Doesn't try hard enough to keep herself looking pretty."

"Oh, brother, that's a cheap thing for him to say," I thought. I looked in the mirror objectively for the first time in years. He was right.

"Oh, well, he was just grasping for something nasty to say," I thought, and went on to the second complaint: "Doesn't have a regular wash day."

"Oh, come on, Danny, get serious. A divorce? Over this?"

The rest of the list was more of the same and made no sense to me at all. Those things seemed so trivial and so unimportant in the whole scheme of things, yet it was all those little things that were ruining our marriage.

It was another five years before *I* changed, but somehow, with the help of God, Danny had decided that *he* would have to be the one to change. He quit criticizing me about the house, he stopped arguing about whose job was whose, and he tried to help me. He would come home from working eight hours, delegate small jobs to the kids, and grab the vacuum cleaner.

I would scurry around with a defensive attitude: "I was GOING to get that done and I would have, too, but ... blah, blah, blah, blah."

"I know you've just got too much to do. I'm not criticizing; I just think you need some help." He stopped trying to change me and accepted me just as I was. By the time we had our third baby he had become mellow and more flexible, and he was always understanding of my good intentions. He gave me the perfect soil and climate in which to grow—love free of conditions and understanding without criticism.

We know that marriage takes more than love. During all those tumultuous first five years, we loved each other, but after we had children and learned how to give more and demand less, after we stopped trying to manipulate the other and decided to accept each other and appreciate all the good we recognized—after we grew up—that's when our marriage started to thrive.

I want to share something with you that I've only recently begun to understand myself. Haven't you heard that love reflects love? That if you give love, you'll get love in return? It has been said, "Whatever you want to receive, *that* is the very thing you must be willing to give." Well, I am a romantic. I love flowers and candy and surprise packages. I longed for Danny to come home from work one day with tickets to someplace exotic. Instead of tickets, he gave me a $30 gift certificate good for Roto-Rooter's next house call. When our last baby was born, he brought flowers to the hospital with a card inscribed, "TO A JOB WELL DONE." The card was signed, "Danny L. Jones."

For anniversaries and birthdays I received things like an automatic weenie cooker or a set of smoke alarms, but never anything personal. Gifts that I gave him were the kind I would have liked myself—but it didn't seem to work in return, according to the promise that "love reflects love."

Before I say anything more, I must tell you that Danny is a wonderful man. He is good and kind, and he loves me and our children beyond anything. All I would have to do would be to complain about the jerky old linoleum in our kitchen and the next day he'd have ripped up the whole floor. If I mention that the handle to my frying pan is wiggly, immediately he's there with a screwdriver, tightening everything in the cupboard. After working all day he comes home and starts working on something around the house that needs fixing. He is always the same (the kind of person you'd like to be next to in an airplane when there's a terrorist on board), always calm, always on top of things, and wise beyond his years, I'm sure.

But it is not natural for him to be gushy or flamboyant. He's too reserved to let his emotions show publicly. It's always been very easy for me, on the other hand, to express my affection for other people. If anything, I've learned how NOT to be so expressive. I've hugged some people spontaneously and felt them shrink with embarrassment. Then I've realized that NOT EVERYBODY LIKES TO BE HUGGED!

Well, here comes the big revelation: There are two different kinds of love—personal love and impersonal love. The first is the kind that I find so easy and natural. It's the one-on-one kind: I grab you and say, "I love you." It's the kind I craved more of. Impersonal love is expressed in different ways. It goes beyond one-on-one; it's given through work and serving others.

Suddenly the light went on. Love reflects love, but personal love returns impersonal love and vice-versa. I had seen it happen in my own marriage and hadn't understood why. Since I'd made the effort to change, to clean up my act and make our home what it was intended to be, I found myself giving more of the impersonal love. (It was as unnatural at first for me as anything unpracticed would be.) I found myself giving my time and energy, and those things returned to me, multiplied. I was loving more, being more, doing more, having more, and it was exhilarating. Something else was happening, which was even more exciting. Danny was beginning to express more personal love. He was more affectionate in ways that I had always hoped he would be.

Recently we were talking about the changes in our marriage that have made it grow into such a beautiful relationship, and Danny said, "You know, I always thought that I loved you much more than you loved me." I couldn't believe my ears!

"How could you ever think that? *I* was always the one to be demonstrative. *I* was the one to take your hand and say, 'I love you.' And you'd just say, 'Thanks.' Didn't you *know* you were the most important person in my life?"

He said, "I heard you *say* those things but then your actions didn't match your words. I thought that if you loved me, then I wouldn't have to go to work hungry and wearing wrinkled clothes. I figured if you really cared, you'd try harder to look as pretty as you were when I married you. I guess I thought all the outward affection and flower talk were superficial."

For the first time I could understand how he'd felt. He saw my change as an expression of love, and he was right. It *was* an expression of love—impersonal love, the kind that's easily recognizable to him, since that's the kind he's always expressed himself.

Today we each practice giving and receiving both kinds of love. After all, it's *all* love, just expressed in two different ways. We accept each other's love *in whatever form it comes,* and in so doing we've reached a balance between personal and impersonal love. He no longer hears my words as superficial because the actions are there to substantiate what I say. I no longer think of his handy work around the house as "convenient," but instead I realize it is his way of showing love for his family. I think of all the years I closed myself off to receiving that love and felt sorry for myself because "I was giving so much more." Ha!

Since I've been organized I asked Danny to tell me in which order of importance he would put the following things: a pretty, clean home; dinner on time; a happy and contented wife.

He said, "I like to come in the back door and hear you singing. Then I like to smell a good dinner, and, finally, I notice how nice the house looks."

In the acknowledgments for this book, Pam and I wanted to put Danny's name first because we both realize that without him, without his support and consideration, we would not have been as free to spread S.H.E. When we have had to meet a self-imposed writing deadline, he has been there to take care of the kids (at times, all six), never complaining about the extra mouths at the table and never feeling threatened by our unique sibling closeness and love. Whenever we've had a problem, his advice has been, "You guys have always made the right decisions in the past. Ask for Divine guidance, and then do what you feel is right."

We will be forever grateful to him, for the freedom and love he has given us.

In telling each of our experiences in marriage, Pam and I have hoped to give you more of ourselves—not to invade the privacy of our families or to embarrass anyone, but to share our feelings with you in the spirit of caring.

My marriage has flourished while my sister's has ended. That may appear to many of you as if one of us has succeeded while the other has failed. Not true!

I can still see my sister's face the day she told me

about the divorce. We both cried and I hugged her. She is shorter than I am, and I thought how small she felt in my arms. I wondered if she'd be weird for a while, as they always are in the movies. I wondered if she'd still laugh and be silly, and I wondered how she could manage alone. I should have known! She is like an iron butterfly. I have marveled at her wisdom and joy through these difficult times. I have seen her vulnerable and under the kind of strain that only a single parent can understand, and I have blessed her.

I know what marriage means to my sister, and I know she didn't casually throw in the towel at the first cross word.

I have an idea that something I said to Sissy just before the marriage broke up prompted the decision. We were talking about how things were going in her marriage, and I said, "Look at it this way: Can't you stay together seven more years? Not till death—that's unreasonable—just seven more years?" Shortly after that conversation we were face to face with the "D" word.

When a marriage ends, the best thing the family can do is offer their home, their company, their food, their food, their food (Sissy eats when she's troubled), and especially their love—not their advice and certainly not their judgment.

It's been a growing experience for all of us, but the children are fine, the dog is fine, Mom and Dad are fine, the neighbors are fine. We're all fine, and life goes on. I love you, Sissy.

FROM BOTH OF US TO YOU

What we all want is more free time—time to do those

things that we were uniquely created to do. We each have a mission in life, and our responsibility to our Creator is to give the best that is in us for the good of all creation. When the house is a mess and you're running off to take the kids to school in your nightgown, you certainly are not in touch with the best that is in you. If your mind is cluttered with the haunting thoughts of all the unfinished jobs you've started, you can't possibly think creatively.

We have received thousands of letters and talked to so many women across the country, and the cry is always the same: "I want more free time." You owe it to *yourself* and then to your family to establish order in your life. If you were born, as we were, with that missing gene, you must realize that, as with any handicap, you have work to do. However, life has its compensation for every handicap that's overcome. We were meant to attain the very best. It is your right to know that you have dominion over your life. You were given the precious gift of choice, and through that power you can do whatever you want to do with your life. Your assets far outweigh your limitations.

Start expecting this system to work. Expect this year to be the greatest year of your life. Step away from all the negative words, the false speculations, and *do not allow* anyone to cause you to doubt your ability to succeed.

When we were within words of completing this book, we paused to contemplate the perfect ending. As we gazed out over a commanding view of the countryside a group of ducks, flying in precision formation, flew overhead. We admired their inner gift of order and self-discipline, instinctively following a path ordained by God. In

silent appreciation we smiled at each other. Then, as we glanced across the horizon, we saw two lone ducks diving and soaring joyously with the wind.

"Do you think they're gonna catch up with the other ducks?"

"I don't think they care if they catch up as long as they end up in the same place. Besides, they're having a ball on the way."

God bless each and every one of you on your way.

Love,

Pam & Peggy

Appendix

Key to Activity List (pp. 136-151)

Frequency
D = Daily
EOD = Every Other Day
2/W = Twice a Week
W = Weekly
EOW = Every Other Week
M = Monthly
EOM = Every Other Month
S = Seasonally
2/Y = Twice a Year
Y = Yearly

Color
Y = Yellow (Daily)
B = Blue (Weekly)
W = White (Monthly)
P = Pink (Personal)

Frequency: How often a job is to be done.
Color: Which color 3×5 card to use for each job.

ACTIVITY LIST

KITCHEN					
Job	Frequency	Time Est.	Mini	Delegate	Color
Dishes					
Wash dishes					
or	D		X		Y
Fill dishwasher					
Empty dishwasher	D		X		Y
Clean dishwasher door	W		X		Y
Wash pots and pans	D		X		Y
Scour sinks	D		X		Y
Polish faucets	D		X		Y
Floors					
Sweep, damp-mop floor	D		X		Y
Wash floor	W				B
Wax floor	M				W
Strip old wax	Y				W
Shake scatter rugs	EOD		X		Y

Cards are filled out with the job, frequency, and time estimate included—one job per card. Cards for jobs taking fewer than ten minutes are marked "Mini."

KITCHEN (contd.)						
Job	Frequency	Time	Est.	Mini	Delegate	Color
Range, Oven						
Scour, drip pans and rims	M			X		W
Clean under drip pans	M			X		W
Clean knobs, clock	M			X		W
Clean range hood	M			X		W
Clean oven inside, outside	M			X		W
Clean microwave in and out	M			X		W
Refrigerator, Freezer						
Defrost freezer	Y					W
Clean inside, outside, top	S					W
Clean drip pan	Y			X		W
Cupboards, Drawers						
Empty and wipe shelves	S					W
Dump anything dead	M					W
Clean cupboard doors	S					W

KITCHEN (contd.)					
Job	Frequency	Time Est.	Mini	Delegate	Color
Wash window over sink	M		X		W
Wash countertops	D		X		Y
Wash canisters, knickknacks	S		X		W
Wash, polish woodwork	S				W
Clean fan	S				W
Wash/dry-clean curtains	Y				W
Clean toaster, can opener/small appliances	M		X		W
Sanitize cutting board	W		X		B
Empty garbage	D		X		Y
Clean under sink	M		X		W
Clean light fixtures	S		X		W
Clean telephone	S		X		W

BATHROOM					
Job	Frequency	Time Est.	Mini	Delegate	Color
Clean tub after each bath	D		X		Y
Clean sink	D		X		Y
Clean toilet	W		X		B
Clean shower stall	M				W
Wash shower curtain	M				W
Wash scatter rugs	M				W
Wash/dry-clean curtains	Y				W
Clean out medicine cabinet	S		X		W
Wash mirror	W		X		B
Wash window	S				W
Clean, polish tile	S				W
Floors Wash floor	W				B
Wax floor	M				W
Strip old wax	S				W
Vacuum carpet	W				B
Shampoo carpet	S				W
Cupboards, Drawers Clean and organize	M		X		W

BATHROOM (contd.)					
Job	Frequency	Time Est.	Mini	Delegate	Color
Clean, polish woodwork	S				W
Polish countertops	W		X		B
Clean brushes, combs	M		X		W
Clean cobwebs	M		X		W

You will need cards for each bathroom.

BEDROOMS					
Job	Frequency	Time Est.	Mini	Delegate	Color
Make bed	D		X		Y
Turn mattress	S		X		W
Wash mattress pad, bedding	EOM		X		W
Clean under bed	S		X		W
Vacuum	W		X		B
Dust/polish furniture	W		X		B
Dust picture frames	W		X		B
Clean closets, drawers	S		X		W
Clean windows (inside)	S		X		W
Clean mirrors	W		X		B
Clean cobwebs	M		X		W

You will need cards for each bedroom.

LIVING ROOM, REC ROOM, DINING ROOM					
Job	Frequency	Time Est.	Mini	Delegate	Color
Vacuum carpet	W		X		B
Shampoo carpet	Y				W
Dust/polish furniture	W		X		B
Rent dump truck to clean fireplace	S				W
Clean windows (inside)	S				W
Dust picture frames	W		X		B
Wash ornaments	S		X		W
Wash/dry-clean curtains, drapes	Y				W
Clean mirrors	W		X		B
Clean light-diffusing bowls	Y		X		W
Move furniture, vacuum under	S				W
Dust lamp shades	W		X		B
Clean walls	Y				W
Clean cobwebs	W		X		B
Clean furnace vents	S		X		W

You will need cards for each room.

Job	Frequency	Time Est.	Mini	Delegate	Color

Extra spaces for additional rooms (library, sewing room, office, etc.) not already listed.

MISCELLANEOUS					
Job	Frequency	Time Est.	Mini	Delegate	Color
Laundry					
Sort, wash, dry, fold, and put away	D				Y
Clean laundry shelves	S				W
Clean laundry-room floor	W				B
Mend, iron	W		X		B
Wash hand washables	W		X		B
Pet care					
Bathe dog	EOM		X		W
Feed dog (cat)	D		X		Y
Clean kitty litter	D		X		Y
Clean bird (hamster) cage	W		X		B
Chores					
Defrost food, prepare meals	D				Y
Set table	D		X		Y
Polish shoes	W		X		B
Plan menu, make grocery list	W				B
Change sheets	W				B
Water plants	2/W		X		Y
Fertilize plants	M		X		W

MISCELLANEOUS (contd.)					
Job	Frequency	Time Est.	Mini	Delegate	Color
Clean fingerprints on light switches	W				B
Dust high places, ledges	W				B
Clean purse	W		X		B
Clean, sweep patio	W		X		B
Sweep porch, walks	W				B
Mow lawn	W				B
Garden	W				B
Clean eaves	S				W
Prune trees	Y				W
Sort seasonal clothing	S				W
Clean out car	W		X		B
Wash car	W				B
Tune up car	2/Y				W
Sort mail	D		X		Y
Write letters	W		X		B
Balance checkbook	D				Y
Do bookkeeping, income tax	M				W
Pay bills	W				B

Put one activity on each card. If the frequency is the same, you may want to group similar activities together (for example, Clean out, wash car).

MISCELLANEOUS (contd.)					
Job	Frequency	Time Est.	Mini	Delegate	Color
Baby Make formula	D		X		Y
Wash bottles, nipples	D		X		Y
Change*	D		X		Y
Bathe	D		X		Y
Clip nails	W				B
Wash clothes	D				Y
Wash diapers	D				Y
Nurse/bottle-feed*	D				Y

Make appointments
    for 6-week, 3-month,
    9-month (etc.)
    checkups					

Small children Bathe	D		X		Y
Wash hair	2/W		X		Y
Dress	D		X		Y
Feed*	D		X		Y
Read stories	D		X		Y

*A 3×5 probably is not necessary, if memory serves us. Babies and small children come with an automatic sounding device.

MISCELLANEOUS (contd.)					
Job	Frequency	Time Est.	Mini	Delegate	Color
Family					
Family council	W				B
Religious Observance	W				B
Children's lessons	D				Y
Candlelight dinner	W				B
Dinner out	M				W
Breakfast out	M				W

PERSONAL ACTIVITIES		
	Day	Frequency
Regular appts.		
Haircut		
Dentist		
Doctor		
Car-pool children		
Classes		
Self-improvement		
College study		
Personal grooming		
Shower, shampoo, makeup		
Shave legs		
Manicure		
Pedicure		
Leisure		
Read		
Study		
Fun shopping		
Lunch out		
Hobbies		
Jogging, exercise		
Wash, starch, iron white uniform; mend hairnet		
Polish white work shoes		

PERSONAL ACTIVITIES (contd.)		
	Day	Frequency
Visiting, Volunteer work Friends		
The elderly		
Shut-ins		
Prisoners, drifters		
Telephoning		
Errands Children's activities		
Banking		
Dry cleaners		
Recycle		
Post office		
Library		
Grocery shopping		
Requests from family		
Car pools		
Go to work		

All personal activities go on pink cards, regardless of frequency.

PERSONAL ACTIVITIES		
	Day	Frequency

SPOUSE'S PERSONAL ACTIVITIES

	Day	Frequency

List additional personal activities not already mentioned.

CHRISTMAS ACTIVITY LIST					
Activity	Start	Time Est.	Mini	Delegate	Finish
Christmas cards bought					
Christmas cards addressed					
Christmas letters written					
Start baking					
Wrap presents for mailing					
Mail Christmas cards and letters					
Mail packages					
Make Christmas decorations					
Get the tree					
Plan Christmas menu					
Put up house lights					
Decorate tree					
Decorate house					
Take children shopping					
Christmas caroling					
Work on church program					
Help plan kids' party at school					
See therapist					

Personalize the list to fit your needs.

GIFTS TO MAKE

Name	Gift	Start	Time Est.	Finish	Wrap
Mom	Quilt	June	4 months	Oct.	X
Dad	Sweater				

GIFTS TO BUY			
Name	Gift	Bought	Wrap

```
┌──────────────────────────────────────────────────────────┐
│              BASIC WEEK PLAN (white card)                │
│  MONDAY       Free Day                                   │
│  TUESDAY      Moderate Cleaning                          │
│  WEDNESDAY    Shop Ads, Clip Coupons                     │
│  THURSDAY     Grocery Shop, Errands                      │
│  FRIDAY       Heavy Cleaning                             │
│  SATURDAY     Children, Family                           │
│  SUNDAY       Church, Family, Free of Cleaning           │
└──────────────────────────────────────────────────────────┘
```

```
┌──────────────────────────────────────────────────────────┐
│              BASIC WEEK PLAN (modified)                  │
│  MONDAY       Moderate Cleaning (2–4 hours)              │
│  TUESDAY      Quiet Day                                  │
│  WEDNESDAY    Groceries                                  │
│  THURSDAY     Moderate Cleaning (2–4 hours)              │
│  FRIDAY       Free Half Day                              │
│  SATURDAY     Moderate Cleaning (2–4 hours)              │
│  SUNDAY       Free                                       │
└──────────────────────────────────────────────────────────┘
```

This Basic Week Plan is a flexible guide to help you spread your work and activities through the week.

```
┌──────────────────────────────────────────────────────────┐
│                MENU PLAN (yellow card)                   │
│  MONDAY       Leftovers/Paper-Plate Night                │
│  TUESDAY      Chicken                                    │
│  WEDNESDAY    Fish                                       │
│  THURSDAY     Casserole/Crock Pot                        │
│  FRIDAY       Hamburgers/Tacos/Spaghetti                 │
│  SATURDAY     Cook's Choice                              │
│  SUNDAY       Feast/Roast/Ham                            │
└──────────────────────────────────────────────────────────┘
```

The Menu Plan coincides with the Basic Week Plan. Use a yellow card and rotate it in the card file, just as you would any other daily cards.

Weekly   Mini   10 min.

SWEEP PATIO WALK
(Children)
Please use broom with red handle in garage. Make
sure gate is locked on patio stairs.

Use a blue card.

Daily   15 min.

FILL DISHWASHER
(Children)
Dishwasher is to be filled after meals. Use Miss See Your
Face dishwasher soap. When dishwasher is filled, turn
machine on.

Use a yellow card.

Monthly   2 hours

WASH AND WAX FAMILY ROOM FLOOR
Vacuum first.
Wash and rinse. Polish.

                                    10/9   10/16
Last done 10/2   Skipped   X   X

This is a monthly card (white) that may be skipped and rescheduled. This card would be a priority on 10/23. See further explanation, pp. 50-53.

JANUARY

Mom and Dad's anniversary   3rd
Martha's birthday   10th
Buzz and Sylvia's anniversary   22nd
Dusty's birthday   25th

CHECK DATES TO REMEMBER

Bongo and Waynette Chrystal Shedlester
1876 North Organized Way
Seattle, Washington 98302

Christmas Cards: Phone: 206-555-8652
Sent:
Received:
Waynette Chrystal collects old TV trays and hates
   to be called Waynee.
Children: Buckeee (yes, 3e's) Dean, 1968;
   Whella Balsom, 1974.
Received birth announcement March 8, 1978.
Baby's name: Whew Ann, weight: 17 lbs., 4 oz.

This is an example of a card that would be filed in the
ABCs. It would be filed in back of *S*.

CHRISTMAS LIST
If you have a sneaky family, call this
    JUNK TO TAKE TO THE DUMP

1. Man's shirt, size large, blue with white collar
2. Baby Heartbeat
3. Nightgown, size small, pink
4. Leather purse, brown
5. Pencil set
6. Clock-radio
7. Cookbook

This Christmas list corresponds to presents that are wrapped and put away. The tag on each present has a number that corresponds to a number on the list.

STORAGE

Seasonal clothing
Furnishings
Party supplies
Wrapping paper, boxes, bows, etc.
Arts-and-crafts supplies
Hand-me-downs (according to age and sex)
Baby equipment
Snow clothes
Sports equipment
Christmas gifts
Christmas decorations
Old toys and books
Easter baskets and decorations
Halloween costumes and decorations

List of suggested things to put into storage so you can streamline the main living area.

STORAGE #C-1

1. Joanna's bathing suit
2. 3 pairs girls' denim shorts
3. Sandals, size 2
4. 3 pairs sunglasses
5. Summer dress, size 5
6. Mike's swimming trunks
7. Girls' swim cover-up
8. Beach towels

This card is for a storage box filled with summer clothes. The box would be stored during the winter when these items are not in use. The box would be marked #C-1 to correspond to the card.

STORAGE #X-8

1. String of blue lights
2. Christmas carolers (ceramic)
3. Santa candy dish
4. Angel hair
5. Christmas cards
6. Christmas napkins
7. Star for top of tree

This card is for a storage box filled with Christmas things; X-8 denotes that it is the eighth box of Christmas things.

JOBS FOR YOUR CHILDREN

You can assign jobs to fit your child's individual capability, since youngsters vary in what they can accomplish at a given age. But don't be afraid to give a child the chance to try or to accept gracefully a little less than perfect performance.

Your three-year-old child needs these 3×5 cards:

Get dressed, put away pajamas
Brush hair
Make bed (will need help)
Fold clothes (washcloths and small articles)
Empty dishwasher (will need help)
Clear meal dishes
Empty wastebaskets
Pick up toys before bed
Story time

Your five-year-old child needs all of the above cards plus:

Set table
Clean bathroom sinks
Help clean and straighten closets and drawers
Clean up after pet
Feed pet (if it doesn't require opening a can)
Dust furniture in room
Vacuum room
Help put groceries away

Your seven-year-old child needs all of the above cards plus:

 Empty garbage
 Sweep walks
 Help in the kitchen after dinner
 Help make lunch for school
 School work
 Clean out car
 Piano lessons, etc.

Your eight-year-old child needs all of the above cards plus:

 Wash bathroom mirrors
 Wash windows
 Wash floors with small areas
 Polish shoes

As your children grow, more responsibility can be given to them. Use your judgment when assigning these jobs:

 Wash car
 Mow lawn
 Make dessert
 Paint
 Clean refrigerator
 Yard work
 Ironing
 Fix an entire meal
 Do the grocery shopping

Visualizations

Because of the nature of our problem, it is most helpful to use our creative imagination in seeing ourselves as we would like to be. These visualizations are exercises in using your creative imagination. They are positive and inspirational and they create an experience that allows you to put yourself in that situation. Their primary purpose is to help the homemaker feel good about herself and her appointment in life.

———

In this perfect moment of now, I let the natural feeling of peace fill me. I realize now that I can change my mind and, in so doing, change my circumstances. As I reflect on the idea that I am in charge of my life through control of my attitude, I find I have more love, more laughter, and

———

greater efficiency in whatever is needed for my chosen career or work.

I thrill at the thought of living another exciting day filled with new ideas, new friendships, and new ways to expand my livingness and all aspects of my life.

In becoming more efficient I am freeing myself to radiate joy and inspire others to tune in on happiness. I want to fulfill my potential as a human being and, in this quiet, peaceful moment, I see myself being the successful person I was made to be.

Today I realize with deep insight that I am a free person. Free to be myself. I need not apologize for what I am. I am not dependent on what other people think. I am free to be me. I love other people and accept them just as they are. In so doing, I am free to love and accept myself.

I realize that being a human being is beautiful and being a homemaker is a wonderful occupation. I am thankful that I have taken this step to improve myself and my home. I can see the entire climate of my home changing for the good. I know I have a lot more to do, but I have come a long way.

The most important thing is that I am happy about the direction my life is taking. I choose to live one day at a time, with the past gone and the future as only a design. I live in the now because that is all that really matters. All the energy and inspiration I need is mine right now and I choose to accept it.

I am an ideal homemaker. I like my appointment in life. I am the heart of my home and I create the climate for all the members of my family. I choose to have a home with a climate of love, peace, joy, beauty, and order.

I am beginning to see the changes I want in my life. I know that I can be just what I set my mind to becoming. Today I look for the good in all the people I meet and every situation I find myself. I love my life and I love who I am, for I am a unique expression of life itself.

There is no other person on earth like me, and my responsibility as a human being is to be a happy, loving, and creative person. All the energy I need to carry out this ideal is already mine and right now I choose to accept it.

I have decided to change and I am pleased with myself. I know that change in my mind must come first and that the tangible effects will naturally follow. I now focus my attention on the good ideas I have about myself. I can be whatever I put my mind to become. . . .

Right now I see myself more beautiful, more understanding, and more patient. I have decided right now that I can be a wonderful homemaker. All the energy I need to accomplish this ideal is now mine. . . . I see myself getting up in the morning full of enthusiasm and joy and I see my family following my example. I see my children cooperating with me and responding well to my love and guidance. In my mind I practice everything such a person would say and do. As I leave this room I carry with me a new and better image of myself. Where there was frustration, now there is a feeling of control. Where there was chaos and disorder, there is a glimmer of hope. I have begun anew and I thank myself for that beginning.

About the Authors

Known for their phenomenally successful books and television appearances, PAM and PEGGY present workshops and provide entertainment for churches, clubs and conventions throughout the country. The sisters have made guest appearances with Oprah, Donahue, Giraldo, Sally Jesse Raphael, Pat Robertson, and Regis. They have been featured in *USA Today*, the *Chicago Times*, the *Christian Science Monitor*, the *Los Angeles Times*, and hundreds of newspapers across the United States. They have cassettes, videos, and personal planners designed to help women get and stay on track. Their materials are woven with humor and point the way to a happier, more rewarding life. If you are interested in obtaining more information or would like to find out about the Sidetracked Sisterhood, which helps S.H.E.s on a personal basis, visit their Web site at www.shesintouch.com or call them at 1-360-696-4091.

Pam and Peggy present mini workshops for churches, clubs and conventions throughout the country. If you are interested in obtaining more information or would like to order the complete home study course on cassette tapes and/or subscribe to the bi-monthly newsletter, *She's On Track*, write or call:

Sidetracked Home Executives™, Inc.

P.O. Box 5364

Vancouver, Washington 98668

(206) 696-4091

THE ORGANIZED EXECUTIVE
The Classic Program for Productivity:
New Ways to Manage Time, Paper, People, and the Digital Office
by Stephanie Winston

REVISED AND UPDATED

Since its first publication two decades ago, this book has become synonymous with success for business professionals everywhere. No other book matches its wealth of ideas for better organization and management. Now, in a special thoroughly revised edition that incorporates the latest digital technology such as e-mail, network servers, handheld computers, and the Internet, here is everything you need to know to adapt your computer to organizing principles.

"A useful and lasting reference."
—Success

GETTING ORGANIZED
The Easy Way to Put Your Life in Order
by Stephanie Winston

Learn how to organize everything in your life—from financial planning to meal planning. Winston shows you how to maximize your storage space, expand your studio apartment, make the most of your new home or office, reduce your shopping time, and increase your efficiency—even how to teach your child to organize too. Long regarded as a business classic, this *New York Times* bestseller has almost half a million copies in print.

"All you need is this book . . . it delivers precisely what it promises."
—Mademoiselle

A WHACK ON THE SIDE OF THE HEAD
How You Can Be More Creative
by Roger von Oech

Filled with provocative puzzles, anecdotes, exercises, metaphors, cartoons, questions, quotations, stories, and tips, this book systematically breaks through your mental blocks and unlocks your mind for creative thinking. It has stimulated creativity in millions of readers and has been used in seminars around the world. Praised by businesspeople, educators, scientists, homemakers, and artists, it can help you break the rules and "think outside the box."

∞